TRADITIONAL **BOX** PROJECTS

TRADITIONAL  BOX PROJECTS

Strother Purdy

The Taunton Press

This book is dedicated to my teachers Rodger Reid and Ed Downs, who taught me more than I'll ever know. Of course everyone else who taught me something is now peeved that I didn't mention them. My apologies. Perhaps if I write enough books I'll get to everyone.

The Taunton Press
Inspiration for hands-on living®

The Taunton Press, Inc., 63 South Main Street, PO Box 5506, Newtown, CT 06470-5506
e-mail: tp@taunton.com

Editor: Courtney Jordan
Copy editor: Seth Reichgott
Indexer: Jim Curtis
Cover design: Teresa Fernandes
Interior design: Susan Fazekas
Layout: Susan Lampe-Wilson
Illustrator: Christopher Mills
Cover and chapter opener photographer: Scott Phillips
Photographer: Strother Purdy

Library of Congress Cataloging-in-Publication Data

Purdy, Strother.
  Traditional box projects / Strother Purdy.
       p. cm.
   ISBN 978-1-60085-110-0
   1. Woodwork. 2. Wooden boxes. I. Title.
  TT200.P78 2010
  684'.08--dc22

                          2009040227

Printed in the United States of America
10 9 8 7 6 5 4 3 2 1

The following manufacturers/names appearing in *Traditional Box Projects* are trademarks:
Blackberry®, Brusso®, Hoffman®, Titebond III®

Working wood is inherently dangerous. Using hand or power tools improperly or ignoring safety practices can lead to permanent injury or even death. Don't try to perform operations you learn about here (or elsewhere) unless you're certain they are safe for you. If something about an operation doesn't feel right, don't do it. Look for another way. We want you to enjoy the craft, so please keep safety foremost in your mind whenever you're in the shop.

Thanks

Heartfelt thanks are due to the peerless **Helen Albert, from whom I've learned much.** But the thanks here are more for publishing this book. And thanks to Jessica DiDonato for her incessantly competent and cheerful assistance. Thanks to the rest of the team at

Taunton for their good work on this book. You'll find all their names deservedly on the facing page.

Larry Neary needs a special thanks, for offering some wood from a very special tree of his for the jewelry box and his help in making it.

I'd also like to thank the roaring economy of 2001 to 2007 for all the work it brought me. I dearly miss you and hope you'll come back soon. What I really mean to say here is a heartfelt thanks to my major patrons, alphabetically to avoid trouble: Meg and Tony Botteon, Stephen and Wanda Brighenti, Joe and Linda Burton, Scott and Joanne Conant, Arthur and Teddy Edelman, Scott and Helene Harrison, Peter and Stephanie Kahane, Bill and Luz MacArthur, Greg and Margaret Oliger, Tom and Elaine Presby, Michael Steiner, and various family members. Your kind words of encouragement and negotiable checks have made it all possible. Thank you.

And thanks to John and Ginny Matchak at the Woodworker's Club and everyone at the Long Island Woodworker's Club for giving me many opportunities to learn something by teaching.

If you feel you should have been acknowledged and weren't, please let me know and we'll include an erratum in subsequent editions.

Contents

  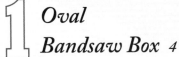      

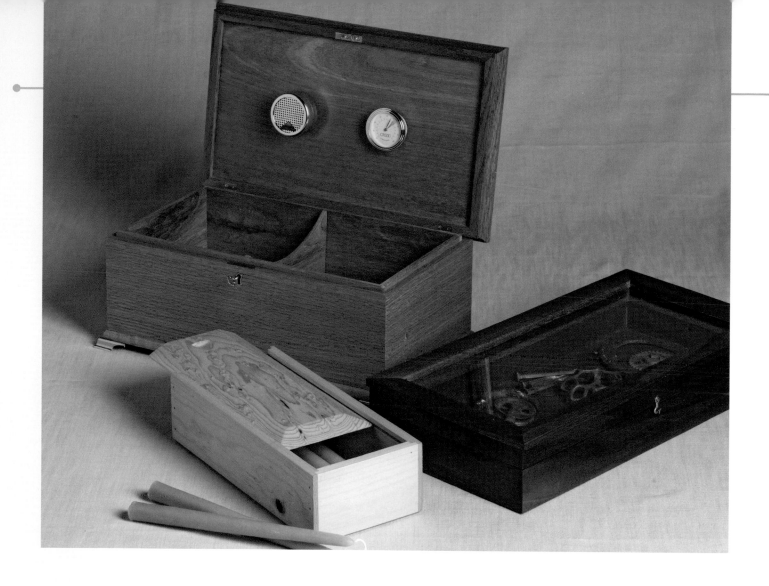

Introduction

The three secrets of making a box are as follows: First, make it well. Second, make it easy. Third, make it beautiful. Yes, these secrets may sound a little disappointing, but they work. And they've worked for millennia.

Making things well ensures they'll last. To know what will last, look to traditional techniques and constructions. They're traditional because they've worked, time and again. The dovetail, the glued edge joint, the rabbet—good joinery doesn't have to be hard to make. It just has to do what's asked of it.

Making things easy is a question of choosing the path of least resistance. A fancy hand-cut mortise and tenon might satisfy the previous rule, but if a biscuit will do, the extra work just makes the job harder. The key, though, is knowing when a biscuit will do, and when it breaks the previous rule.

Making things beautiful is the most important rule. Beauty sounds quite mysterious, even intangible. But if something is made well, you're halfway there. The other half is just as easy when you plunder the treasure trove of forms that's called tradition.

These are the shapes, patterns, and colors that you find time and again in the great works of art and craft throughout history. The distilled concepts include the S-curve, graduated series, and symmetry. With them you can make a table with cabriole legs, a dresser with bigger drawers on the bottom, a box with handles on both ends.

Some woodworkers equate tradition with a stifling set of rules that they itch to break. If it has always been made that way, they have to make it differently to explore their individuality. We should be thankful for this itch—it fuels the innovations that become tradition. Long ago, all ideas were new ideas, but some of them worked so well that others adopted them. The trouble is that the vast majority of innovations are failures, even if some last for a generation or two. It's the rare innovation, the rare genius, which persists. So when we work with the proven tools of traditions we have, by far, the greatest chance of making something lasting and beautiful.

This isn't a book of reproductions. Every project in this book is unique. And yet I lay no claim to inventing anything here. All these designs have strong roots in the work of other, better woodworkers. The Shaker lap desk and the book boxes are very close to their originals. Others, such as the jewelry box, are more interpretations of traditional elements. I invite you to bring the same spirit to your work. If you like, copy one of these boxes as closely as you can. Or use only what you want—

a design idea here, a technique there—and otherwise fill the brevity of the form with the richness of your imagination. I've strived to write a book that's as helpful as it can be, as clear as it can be, and as enjoyable as I'm able to make it.

When you first start out, woodworking looks like a set of stairs and you're at the bottom. With time and hard work, you can "make it to the top." But after a few years of practice, woodworking starts to look more like a maze, or a "garden of forking paths." Each project starts as a series of options (what wood to use? what exact dimensions?). The decisions for each question create a new set of options, and so on. I've been lost in this garden many times, and I've taken the wrong paths occasionally. But there's always a way out; the project always gets finished. If you find I've taken any wrong turns in this book, I freely admit the mistakes, and ask you to please forgive them.

After years of making things, many woodworkers forget how hard it was at first. In part because years of accumulated tooling means we always have the right tool for the job. But that's not the case for everyone, so I've tried to keep the tool kit to a minimum and offer options. Years of practice means we make things without thinking. And making hands explain themselves is tough to do. If you follow the instructions and it still doesn't come out like in the book, it's just a matter of practice until you do. Your hands will learn far more by practice than by reading.

1 Oval Bandsaw Box

In some ways a bandsaw box makes a misleading introduction to box making. They're simply not like other boxes, requiring an almost totally different set of tools and in no need of any type of joinery except glue. So if you're looking for traditional box construction, skip to the next chapter. No, wait. Stick around in this chapter. I take that all back.

Bandsaw boxes are utterly cool because they look like a solid piece of wood. There's no apparent joinery and no apparent seams between pieces (there really are, but don't tell anyone). And making them is so much fun it can become all-consuming. Once you discover for yourself that they're really easy to make, it can be hard to stop. They look beautiful, can be made in nearly any shape, and make fantastic gifts. What more to ask? However, there is the danger that you'll end up on a craft show circuit selling them for a living.

This project is a simple, medium-size oval box, and a good place to start. With practice you can try more adventurous forms, both larger and smaller, as the technique lends itself to creativity. A visit to a craft show will let you see some of the possibilities with the form. I've kept this box deliberately simple. Add a top knob or line the bottom, if you like, using techniques shown in other chapters.

Aside from the typical assortment of clamps, saws, and other shop tools, you'll need (of course) a bandsaw, a drill press with sanding drums, and a French curve to lay out the oval. Flexible sanding pads are also really helpful to sand the curves, but you can get along without them.

OVAL BANDSAW BOX

Four slices from a piece of maple are all that make up this bandsaw box. You create the box cavity by sawing out the middle section.

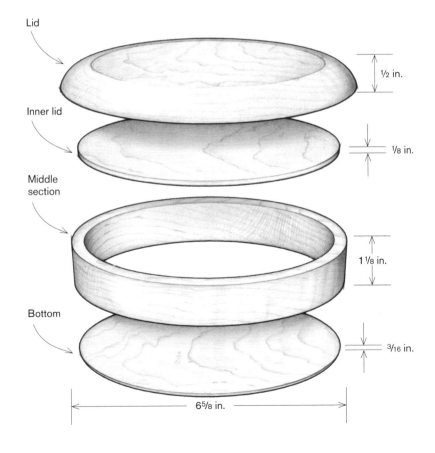

Lid — ½ in.

Inner lid — ⅛ in.

Middle section — 1⅛ in.

Bottom — ³⁄₁₆ in.

6⅝ in.

Mill an Oversize Block

1. Start with a block of wood bigger than you need. If you're going to take the box from the end of a plank, don't cut your block to rough dimensions just yet.

2. If your wood is rough milled, then joint one face flat on a jointer.

3. Plane the opposite face to a final thickness of $1\frac{7}{8}$ in. or more.

work SMART

If you don't have stock thick enough, glue two or more pieces together face-to-face. However, the non-continuous grain might not give you the look you want.

Laying Out an Oval

You can't lay out an oval with a compass (unless you're really sloppy). For a true ellipse, or a mathematically symmetrical oval, you're on your own. But here's a simple technique to create a very nice oval with a French curve meant for drafting.

1. Draw a cross at least the length and width of the box you want. I use a drafting triangle because a combination square won't lay flat on the board.

2. Align the French curve edge between the two endpoints of one quadrant of the cross. Slide it around to find the line that looks right. You should avoid laying out a shape with sharp transitions. When you get the right look, draw it on that quarter. Mark the start and end of the line on the French curve with pieces of tape. Lay out this same curve on the other three quadrants of the cross using the tape as guides. Now you have an oval outline. **A**

3. Crosscut and rip the oval from the larger board if necessary. The idea is to make your block a rectangle just bigger than the oval shape of the box. **B**

A

LAY OUT AN OVAL on the board with a French curve. Mark the curve for one quarter of the oval with tape, then transfer the same section to the other quarters.

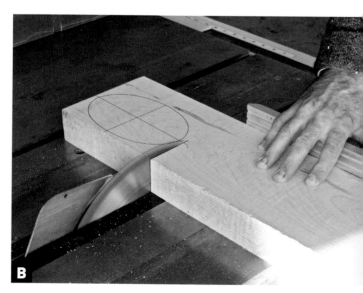

B

TRIM THE BOARD TO SIZE on the tablesaw, just larger than the oval itself.

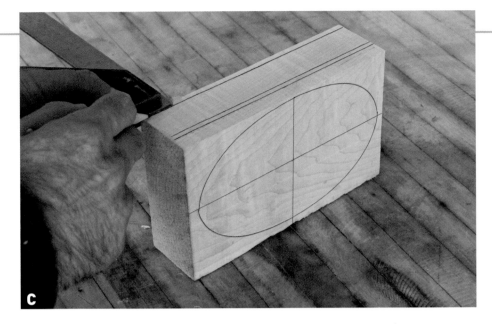

MARK THE CUT LINES FOR RESAWING the box sections with a pencil and combination square.

4. Scribe lines on one edge that show where to cut the bottom piece, middle section, and two lid pieces. I use a combination square and pencil, but a marking gauge will also work fine. The thicknesses (and layout line locations) are as follows: $3/16$ in. bottom, $1\frac{1}{8}$ in. middle section, $1/8$ in. inner lid, and $1/2$ in. lid. **C**

5. Most important, draw a triangle for orientation on one side of the block. This is crucial to avoid confusing the relationship of the pieces. The triangle shape is best because it's nearly impossible to confuse one end for the other. **D**

Sawing the Box into Layers

Resawing curved shapes on a bandsaw can be very dangerous. The workpiece can be caught and spun by the blade. So resaw your box into layers before you cut the oval profile.

1. Fit a wide ($5/8$-in. or $3/4$-in.) blade in your bandsaw. It's possible to resaw the block with a smaller blade, but not as easy. You'll have to go much more slowly and watch that the blade doesn't wander from the line of cut. And the more it wanders, the more sanding you'll have to do.

DRAW A TRIANGLE ON THE EDGE of the box blank so you can orient the parts after you've sawn them apart.

2. Set up the bandsaw's fence $3/16$ in. from the blade. You don't need a special resawing fence to cut such a small block, though it might help.

3. Saw each piece from the block. I tend to saw down the middle of the layout lines rather than to one side or the other. Just make sure you're consistent so you don't make any one piece thinner at the

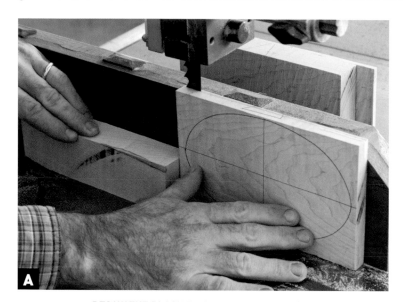

RESAW THE BLOCK INTO LAYERS on a bandsaw. For small blocks, the regular fence will work fine. Use a push block to keep your fingers away from the blade.

expense of another. Use a push block when sawing the block into pieces. Without one, your fingers can get too close to the blade. **A**

4. After each cut, make a light pass on the jointer to smooth the face of the block. This will make sure you have one smooth face on each layer. You can't easily joint the faces of the thin layers after you've cut them from the block. **B**

5. When you've sawn all four pieces, smooth the rough face of each to 100 or 120 grit. Ideally, use a thickness sander that can handle small pieces. If you have neither, then you're stuck sanding by hand, like me. This can be tricky work. Random-orbit sanders tend to be more aggressive at the edges of small workpieces, which leads to domed surfaces. A hard sanding pad and some care will keep the pieces flat enough.

JOINT THE FACE OF THE BLOCK after each cut. This ensures you have one flat face on each piece.

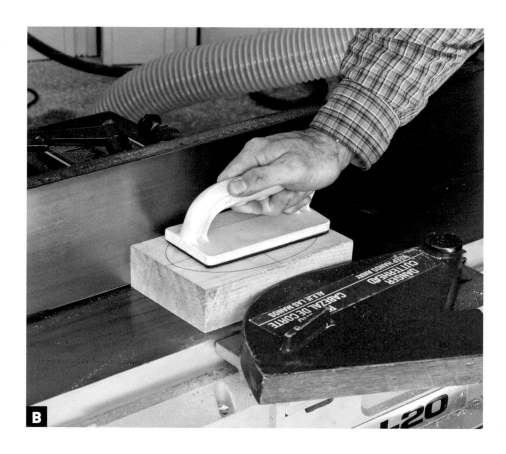

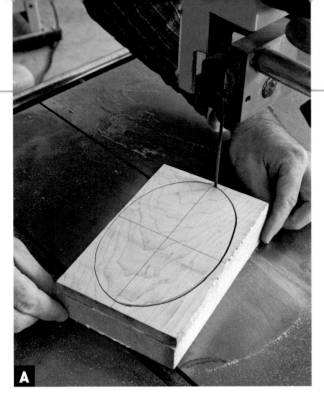

A

SAW THE OVAL PROFILE on all four layers at once, stacked and taped together. Use a thin bandsaw blade to cut the curves.

B

SAND THE EDGES OF THE BOX smooth while the parts are still taped together.

Sawing the Oval

1. Fit a narrow ($\frac{1}{4}$-in. or $\frac{3}{8}$-in.) blade in your bandsaw to cut the oval curves; a wider blade can't cut a tight enough radius.

2. Stack and secure the four pieces together with double-sided tape between each piece so they don't move against one another while you saw and sand them. Test the tape joint before you start to saw.

3. Saw the outline of the oval on the bandsaw. It's best to make one continuous cut rather than several because the edge will be smoother and easier to sand. **A**

4. With the four pieces still taped together, sand the outside edges of the box. The best tool for this is a stationary belt sander because it holds the box exactly 90 degrees to the sanding belt. If you don't have one, sand however you like, but make sure that you sand the sides perpendicular to the faces. The oval outline can start to look a bit lumpy if you don't. **B**

C

DRAW ANOTHER ORIENTING TRIANGLE on the side before disassembling the stacked layers.

5. Because you cut away the orienting triangle mark, make another one on the side of your sanded oval. **C**

DRAW A LAYOUT LINE ³⁄₈ IN. around the inside of the middle layer. Using your finger against a pencil as a guide works well.

Sawing the Interior

This cut looks difficult because you're cutting on an inside line. Just go slowly and you'll find it rather simple.

1. Remove the double-sided tape and separate the pieces. Draw a line along the edge of the middle layer, ³⁄₈ in. to ⁵⁄₁₆ in. from the outside edge. There are fancy marking gauges designed for curved edges (they have two pins for a fence instead of a flat block). Use one if you have one. As I don't, I find using my finger as a gauge works just fine. Just set the pencil firmly in your hand (hey, the hand is the most versatile tool around) so the tip is the right distance from the edge, and allow your finger to guide the pencil around the wood. **A**

2. Saw out the center of the oval on the bandsaw. It's important to start the cut at one of the ends and not in the sides. The reason is that you'll glue the gap back together, and a cut at the end gives you a face-grain to face-grain joint. **B**

SAW OUT THE WASTE AT THE CENTER of the middle section on the bandsaw. Start the cut at one end, not along a side.

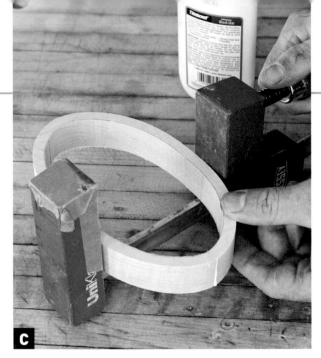

C

GLUE THE ENTRY KERF JOINT back together with yellow glue. Light clamping is essential to avoid distorting the glue joint.

D

SAND THE INTERIOR OF THE BOX on a drill press fitted with a sanding drum.

3. Remove the waste from the middle and glue the kerf where you started the cut back together. Technically your oval is now thinner at one end, but the difference is miniscule because the closed gap is so small. Clamp with gentle pressure, as you can easily bow the sides and distort the glue joint surfaces. **C**

4. When the glue is dry, sand the interior of the middle layer. The best tool for the job is a drill press with sanding drum attachment because it can sand curves evenly at 90 degrees to a surface. Your other options are limited. A detail sander with a curved head might work if it fits inside the box. Sanding by hand is very difficult because the curves are tight. Flocking or using adhesive-backed lining are both ways to avoid sanding the interior. But leaving it unsanded will look distinctly sloppy. **D**

5. The inner lid needs to fit into the middle layer. Mark your line of cut by tracing the middle layer's

interior edge on the inner lid. Saw along the line using the bandsaw. As the wood is thin, use extra caution to avoid cracking or breaking the piece. **E**

6. Now sand the inside faces of the bottom and top pieces. You should do it now because after you glue them up, the surfaces aren't as easily accessible and are very hard to sand.

E

MARK THE LINE OF CUT on the inner lid using the middle layer as a guide.

Assembly

There's really no joinery in this bandsaw box to speak of except glued joints.

GLUE THE INNER LID TO THE BACK of the lid and clamp all around. Watch the glue line for gaps and clamp them as necessary.

1. Glue the inner lid to the bottom of the lid. As the bottom is thin and flexible, you want to get clamping pressure at all points. A half dozen or more small clamps works best, I think, as cauls can hide spots where the two don't touch. To align the inner lid properly, use the middle section in place as a guide (before you apply clamps). **A**

work SMART

As you clamp the box parts together, watch that they don't slide out of position. Yellow glue is slippery, so parts can shift until clamped firmly together.

GLUE THE MIDDLE SECTION to the bottom. Use as many clamps as you can fit to ensure a tight glue joint.

work SMART

For best results, clean off beads of glue that squeeze out after the glue becomes rubbery but before it hardens.

2. Glue the box bottom to the middle section using the same style of clamping. Be sure to check the orienting triangle on the side to get alignment right. Let the glue set. **B**

Finishing

1. It's best to shape and sand the exterior of the box as a single unit. So tape the lid and bottom together with bits of double-sided tape. **A**

2. Sand the outside edges of the box on a stationary belt sander. Finish up with a hand sander, orbital, or random orbital. You should sand before routing to get a smoother routed edge.

WITH DOUBLE-SIDED TAPE, secure the lid to the box before routing or sanding the exterior.

ROUND OVER THE TOP AND BOTTOM EDGES on a router table. Be careful to push the workpiece through the cut, against the direction of the bit.

3. Round over the edges of box, top and bottom, on a router table fitted with a bearing-guided roundover bit. Don't try this with a handheld router. The box is small and nearly impossible to clamp, making disaster likely. Even on the router table, hold the box very securely and push it through the cut, against the spinning direction of the bit. **B** If you don't have a router table, you can either leave the edges straight (looks like a Shaker oval box) or file down the edges with a rasp. Using a rasp just takes more time and an eye for accuracy.

4. Finish sanding the box's exterior. This job is awkward business and best done by hand. The box is small and only the top and bottom are flat. Simply using a quarter-sheet of sandpaper does the job. However, I've had the best success with flexible sanding blocks. They conform to the curved edges well and last longer than sandpaper. Sand up to 220 grit or more for maple. **C**

5. For finishing, either an oil or wipe-on varnish works well.

FINISH SANDING THE EXTERIOR of the box with sanding sponges that conform to its curves.

 # Shaker Candle Box

have two candle boxes in my house, neither for candles. One holds loose change, like a piggy bank. The other keeps pencils and pens. A friend uses one for receipts—they go from his wallet into the box every day, where they stay until he summons the courage to record and file them. Until then, he looks at a nice box instead of a stack of paper.

Before the appearance of light bulbs, candle boxes held candles, a primary source of household light after dark. But candle boxes have evolved into simple, small storage boxes for everything from poker chips and seashells to drink coasters and bulk spices.

Whatever you make a candle box for, tailor the interior dimensions accordingly. Make the interior big enough to hold what you want, then add space to fit a finger inside to pull the contents out. This candle box is a few inches wider and longer than a business envelope. I'll use it for pencils and pens. Then again, my daughter may take it for her rubber lizard collection.

Historically, Shaker candle boxes have ranged from simple and crude construction with butt joints and nails to more sophisticated designs with elegant dovetails. The design of this one comes from no particular candle box, but a mixture of several. The rabbeted and nailed corners are easy to build and attractive. The sliding top with a carved finger pull is straightforward and practical. Pine is easy to work and wears gracefully. Use it daily, and the box will take on a nice patina within a year. You can find dimensioned white pine at most lumberyards. The #2 grade is cheap, but will give you knots that are hard to work (though they have an interesting look). Clear white pine is more expensive, but for a small box project it won't dent the wallet badly.

SHAKER CANDLE BOX

The construction of this box is a combination of simple grooves and rabbets. The sliding top is beveled and has a finger pull carved at one end. The rabbeted corners are nailed. The box rests on the bottom panel, not the edges, as the groove is set ⅜ in. from the bottom edge and the panel is ½ in. thick. The box consequently looks like it floats above the surface it is set on.

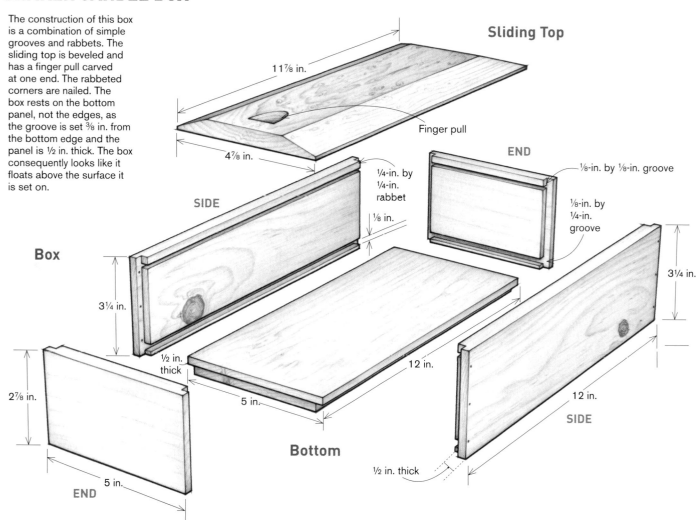

Sliding Top

11⅞ in.

Finger pull

4⅞ in.

END

⅛-in. by ⅛-in. groove

¼-in. by ¼-in. rabbet

⅛ in.

⅛-in. by ¼-in. groove

SIDE

Box

3¼ in.

3¼ in.

½ in. thick

12 in.

12 in.

SIDE

2⅞ in.

5 in.

Bottom

½ in. thick

END

5 in.

MATERIALS

Quantity	Part	Actual Size	Construction Notes
2	Sides	½ in. by 3¼ in. by 12 in.	White pine
1	Bottom	½ in. by 5 in. by 12 in.	White pine
2	Ends	½ in. by 3¼ in. by 5 in.	White pine; one end is ripped to 2⅞ in. wide
1	Top	½ in. by 4⅞ in. by 11⅞ in.	White pine
12	3d nails or decorative brads		3d nails clipped to ⅞ in. long

CHECKING FOR WARPS IN SMALL STOCK

When checking if small stock is warped, looking down the board can sometimes fool the eye. There just isn't enough distance to gauge the warp. And twists are nearly impossible to see. But set the board on a very flat surface, such as a jointer bed, and you'll be able to tell instantly. A twisted board will rock from corner to corner. On a bowed or cupped board, you'll be able to see where it touches the table and where it doesn't. No squinting necessary.

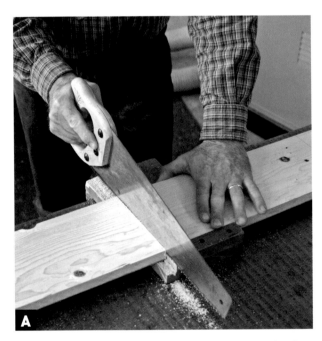

USE A CROSSCUT SAW AND BENCH HOOK to cut your lumber to oversize lengths.

Prep Work

Commercially dimensioned lumber is rarely straight and flat. For a small box, the parts don't have to be perfect. But the closer you can get, the better. Also look for pieces with interesting figure. I found a board with a little bird's-eye figure at one end to use for the top.

1. Crosscut your boards to oversize lengths, an inch or two longer than the finished dimensions. However, don't cut the ends to rough length just yet. They would be too short to joint and plane. So leave them as a single 12-in. piece until you cut final dimensions in a later step. **A**

B

RIP THE BOARDS TO ROUGH, oversize widths on a table-saw. For boards over 3 in. in width, it is safer to use your hand than a push stick.

2. Rip the boards ¼ in. wider than their final dimensions. **B**

3. Joint one face of each of the boards. If they're flat from the lumberyard, then don't bother with this step. **C**

4. Plane all the boards to about ⁹⁄₁₆ in. thick.

C

JOINT THE FACE OF EACH BOARD flat and true. Use a push block when face-jointing small pieces.

FLATTENING MILLED STOCK

Jointing a bow or twist from a roughsawn board is much easier than doing it from a milled board. The reason is because you can easily see where you're cutting—the roughsawn face contrasts with the smooth jointed face. On a milled board, it's hard to see where you're cutting and where you're not. You can hear that you're cutting the board, but the sound doesn't tell you where the cut is made.

Scribbles with a pencil solve this problem easily. Just draw across both faces. As you joint, the pencil lines will stay on the higher parts. When you've gotten rid of all the pencil lines, you've made a fully engaged cut.

5. Stack the boards on edge with space between each. Let them sit overnight or longer. This gives any internal stress a chance to express itself before you mill the parts to final dimension. **D**

6. In the morning, check the boards for warping. Re-joint the faces flat again if needed. Otherwise skip this step.

7. Plane the stock down to the final ½ in. thickness.

8. Joint one edge square on each of the boards. Then rip the opposite edge of each board to final width. Remember that the sides and ends should be 3¼ in. wide, the bottom should be 5 in. wide, and the top should be 4⅞ in. wide. You'll cut the one end down to 2⅞ in. later. **E**

9. Before you crosscut your pieces to final length, check that your tablesaw's miter gauge is accurately at 90 degrees (unplug the saw before checking). It surprises me how often and easily miter gauges go out of square, so it's good insurance to check before every use. **F**

EDGE JOINT EACH PIECE HELD TIGHTLY against the fence. On small pieces, mind your fingers—never go below the guard.

BEFORE CROSSCUTTING, CHECK THAT YOUR MITER GAUGE and blade are at 90 degrees. Mind that the blade of the square fits snugly against the face of the sawblade and isn't skewed against a tooth.

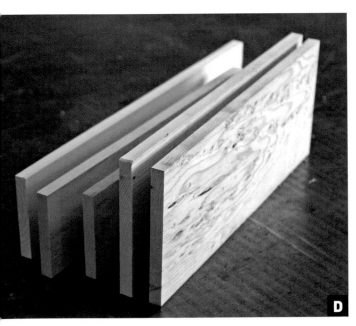

LET THE ROUGH MILLED BOARDS stand on edge overnight, with airspace between them, to release stresses. Stack them out of the way.

USE A STOP BLOCK CLAMPED to the miter gauge to ensure you crosscut the two ends and two sides exactly the same length.

10. Crosscut each piece to length. For the sides and ends, it pays to use a stop block. This helps ensure both pieces are the same length and that your box will be rectangular. **G**

Cutting the Rabbets

Rabbet joints are easy to make on a tablesaw. You use the rip fence and miter gauge simultaneously. When you cut through a board, this is a recipe for a kickback. But as you're not cutting through boards, this combination isn't any more dangerous than usual tablesaw use. It's also possible to cut the rabbets by hand if you prefer.

1. Orient the sides and ends the way you want them when the box is finished. Label each joint with letters or numbers (or cryptic symbols if you like). Pine dents easily, so use a light touch or your marks will be hard to sand out. Most helpful, label the outside face of each piece (I write "out"). These markings will help you avoid the mistake of cutting the rabbets on the wrong side of the board. **A**

2. I scribe rabbets with a marking gauge even when cutting them on the tablesaw. It gives a clear indication of where the cuts should be and, again, helps me avoid mistakes. Scribe the ¼-in. by ¼-in.

WRITING LETTERS OR NUMBERS TO INDICATE matching joints helps avoid mistakes. For the same reason, write "out" on the outside of the boards.

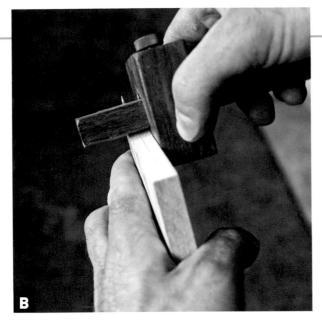

B

SCRIBE A LINE ALONG THE EDGE of each board with a marking gauge to describe the rabbet, ¼ in. from the inside face.

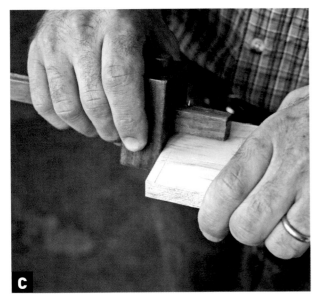

C

SCRIBE A LINE ON THE INSIDE FACE of each side and end, ¼ in. from the edge.

rabbets on the inside of the side pieces, first along the edge, **B** then along the face. **C**

3. Fit your tablesaw with a rip or dado blade if you have either, as a sawblade with a flat-topped tooth profile produces the best rabbet. However, you can use a common ATB profile blade, which cuts a V-shaped kerf. You just have to clean up the cut with a shoulder plane afterward (that's what I did).

4. Set the blade just less than ¼ in. high. If the blade cuts a ⅛-in. kerf, then set your fence just less than ⅛ in. from the blade (the blade kerf and distance to the fence should add up to ¼ in.). Make test cuts with a piece of scrap until you cut perfect ¼-in. by ¼-in. rabbets.

work
SMART

Before you make a cut, check the marks you've made on your workpieces. Their job is to remind you of the proper orientation when there's an opportunity to make a mistake. And every cut is an opportunity for a mistake.

5. It will take two passes to cut the rabbet with a ⅛-in. blade. For the first cut, the workpiece should be tight to the fence. For the second cut, move the workpiece ⅛ in. away from the fence, essentially flush with the blade. **D**

D

CUT THE RABBETS USING THE MITER GAUGE and the rip fence. The workpiece should be tight to the rip fence and the miter gauge on the first pass.

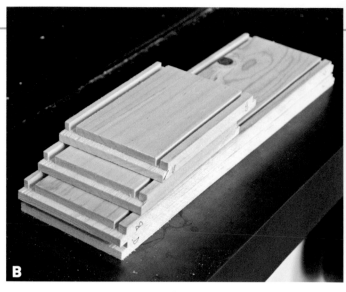

THE RABBETS AND GROOVES should be the same depth.

RIP THE GROOVE FOR THE CAPTURED BOTTOM with two passes, adjusting the rip fence between each cut.

Cutting the Grooves

The tablesaw is also the best tool to cut the grooves for the captured bottom and sliding top. The kerf does not need a flat bottom, so using an ATB blade is fine.

1. After cutting the rabbets, leave the blade height at $1/4$ in. Set the rip fence $1/4$ in. from the blade.

2. Rip the $1/8$-in.-wide groove for the top on both side pieces and only one end piece (see step 4 for the other end piece).

3. Rip the $1/4$-in. groove for the captured bottom with two passes (unless you're using a dado blade). Move the fence $1/8$ in. after the first pass. Your grooves and rabbets should be the exact same depth. **A & B**

4. Raise the blade and reset the rip fence on the tablesaw to $2 7/8$ in. from the blade and rip the second end piece. The top edge of the end piece should align with the bottom of the groove on the side pieces. This cut allows the top to slide in and out of the finished box.

Make the Bottom

The bottom is captured in the groove on the ends and sides. To fit it, you simply cut a $1/4$-in. by $1/4$-in. rabbet on all the edges. The ends can be rabbeted the same way as the joints shown previously (see p. 20). The following steps show how to cut rabbets on the sides of boards, which you shouldn't do with a miter gauge.

1. Mark the $1/4$-in. by $1/4$-in. rabbet on the edges and ends of the side boards with a marking gauge.

CUT AN $1/8$-IN. GROOVE ON THE OUTSIDE face of the bottom.

2. Set the tablesaw rip fence ⅛ in. from the blade. Set the blade height to ¼ in.

3. Rip grooves on the outside face (the face that will be outside of the box when assembled). **A**

4. Cut grooves on the ends using the miter fence as a guide. **B**

B

CUT THE GROOVE ON THE ENDS using the miter gauge for stability.

5. Finish the rabbets on the ends by pulling the workpiece away from the rip fence and cutting away the waste. This is how you cut the rabbet joints. However, this technique won't work for cutting the rabbets along the edges. Therefore, reset the rip fence ¼ in. from the blade and run the workpiece on edge against the rip fence. **C**

6. If the rabbet is too thick to fit in the groove easily, use a shoulder plane to shave it down and use a bench hook to hold the piece (see p. 26). Take light passes and check the fit often until each side and each end fits snugly into the appropriate groove. **D**

C

RIP THE WASTE FROM THE RABBET by running the workpiece on edge, tight to the rip fence.

D

TRIM AN OVERSIZED RABBET with a shoulder plane. Use a bench hook to secure the workpiece.

Assembly

Rabbets do not make a strong glue joint, as there is no face-grain to face-grain connection. Glue helps quite a bit, but nails do most of the long-term connecting work. So after you glue the box together, handle it gingerly until you've set the nails.

1. Sand the inside faces of the four sides and the bottom piece before assembly. Although I used a random-orbit sander, a block and sandpaper does as good a job (it just takes more time). I started with 180 grit and finished with 220 grit because there were no major tearouts in the grain and pine is soft and cuts quickly. Use a pad (I used squares of rattan) to protect the backs of the workpieces as you sand. **A**

2. Before final assembly, I highly recommend clamping the parts together dry to see that everything fits. This doesn't take more than five minutes, and may save you from starting over if anything is seriously mismatched. Use a shoulder plane to trim the rabbets (as you did for the bottom) if they don't fit tightly.

3. Dab a light layer of glue on the surface of each rabbet, though not where the top intersects. Resist the temptation to put glue in the grooves. Although the bottom might not crack on such a small box, you'll surely end up with lots of glue squeeze-out to clean up. **B**

USE A STICK OR BRUSH TO DAB GLUE along the two faces of each rabbet. Be careful not to get glue in the grooves.

4. Lightly clamp the box sides, ends, and bottom together and check that every part lines up right. Check the diagonal measurements and realign the clamps if they are not equal. **C**

5. When you have everything just right, fit clamps snugly lengthwise and widthwise across the box. Try to do this all very quickly before your glue sets, usually under five minutes with a standard PVA adhesive. If you prefer working in a relaxed manner, use a glue with a slower set, such as Titebond III®. **D**

6. Unclamp the box after about 30 minutes. Inspect the inside of the box for any glue squeeze-out and remove it while it's still rubbery, though not liquid. Dry glue is far harder than pine. This makes it nearly impossible to remove without tearing the wood. **E**

7. Let the glue cure for a day or two. Then sand all surfaces up to 220 grit, being careful not to stress the joints with too much pressure.

SAND THE INSIDE SURFACES OF THE BOX up to 220 grit before assembly. Use a pad to protect the soft pine from the work surface.

CHECK THE DIAGONAL MEASUREMENTS from each opposite corner during clamping. Adjust the clamps to ensure both diagonals are equal before applying full pressure.

APPLY CLAMPS ACROSS THE LENGTH and the width of the box to hold the rabbets tightly against each other.

Bevel and Fit the Top

I find it difficult to choose what kind of top to make for these boxes. There are many choices, each with their pros and cons. The rabbet joints leave a notched edge, which I like to hide with a flush-fitting top. But a beveled top is far easier to make and nicer looking.

1. Mark out the bevel edge on the top piece with a scribed line about ¹⁄₁₆ in. from the bottom edge. This line will help you keep an even thickness for the edge. **A**

USE A SHARP CHISEL TO REMOVE glue squeeze-out while it's still rubbery. If it dries hard, you risk tearing the wood.

work SMART

As pine dents easily, take care what you rest your box on. If your work surface isn't perfectly clean, another piece of pine makes a good backer to avoid marring your freshly sanded box. Rubbery or soft mats won't mar, but setting the nails will be a real chore, as the hammer will bounce back.

WITH A MARKING GAUGE, SCRIBE A LINE ¹⁄₁₆ in. along the edges of the top.

2. Draw a line about 1 in. from the edge along three sides of the face. The unmarked side is where the finger pull will go, so choose that now. This line will determine the slant of the bevel. If you want a sharper-angled bevel, mark a line closer to the edge. **B**

WITH A COMBINATION SQUARE set to 1 in., mark a line around three sides of the top. This determines the angle of the bevel along the edges.

B

MAKING A BENCH HOOK

MAKING A BENCH HOOK takes a little time, some scrapwood, a little glue, and a few clamps to create a tool that will be useful for many years.

PUSH YOUR WORKPIECE AGAINST THE BACK of the bench hook when sawing.

A bench hook is simply a board with a cross-piece at either end. That it should be so simple belies its huge versatility as a holding tool. Its primary use is for crosscutting boards and trimming tenons. But it's also very useful for other hand-tool work. Throughout this book, you'll see it in action many times. Here I'll show you how to make one and some general tips on using it.

You just need a flat and square scrap, 5 in. to 9 in. wide and 10 in. to 12 in. long, for a good base. If you use a piece that is too small, it won't hold large workpieces well. Much bigger, and the jig takes up too much space. Two pieces about ¾ in. square glued and

screwed to both short ends, on either side of the base, complete the jig.

The only construction detail is that the crosspiece on top should be a little shorter than the base is wide. Attach it flush with the left of the base piece (or the right if you're a left-hander). This allows the board to act as a backer when sawing, so you never cut into your bench.

To use the hook, align the bottom cross piece with the edge of the bench, or even clamp it in a vise. Put your workpiece on the hook and lean on it as you work. If the workpiece moves, lean forward on it harder.

CUT THE BEVEL WITH A BLOCK PLANE, angling it to cut evenly toward the pencil line on the top and the scribe line along the edge.

TEST THE FIT OF THE TOP in the groove periodically as you cut the bevels.

USE A PENCIL TO MARK WHERE YOU SHOULD remove material from the bevel end for a better fit.

3. Using a bench hook as a stay (see "Making a Bench Hook" on the facing page), bevel one end first, then the two sides. You should work in this order because you can get tearout at the end of the crosscut. When you bevel the sides, you cut away the tearout. I use a block plane, **C** though a sander with 80-grit paper will also work.

4. Test the fit of the top as you go. You want a snug fit (though not very tight) at this point.

After sanding, the top will slide more easily. Try to remove equal amounts from the two sides so the bevels are symmetrical. **D**

5. Check the fit of the end to see if the top fits evenly into the groove. Rub a pencil on the bevel where it's high, then either use the block plane or sandpaper to adjust the fit. **E**

Carve the Finger Pull

I've seen nice finger pulls in many different sizes and shapes, so there's no one way to do it. This one is a rounded acorn shape that's a bit bigger than my finger. You'll need a gouge to cut this one. Although I used a 12mm #5 straight gouge, almost any gentle sweep will do. So use what you have and make one to your own taste.

1. Mark the shape of the finger pull with a pencil. Practically speaking, it should have a deep end near the end of the top. This makes it easy for your finger to get a grip and pull the top open.

2. With the top on the bench hook, push or tap small cuts at a steep angle toward the end. Too much enthusiasm can break a chip all the way through to the end, so go lightly. **A**

LIGHTLY CUT CHIPS (tap with a hammer if you prefer) at a steep angle to start the finger pull. The bench hook makes an excellent stay for the workpiece.

B

CHOP DOWN TO BREAK OUT the chips you started. The gouge may leave marks at the bottom of the finger pull, but they make the box handmade.

3. At the back of the finger pull, chop out the chips you started. **B**

4. Sand the top to 220 grit as you did for the other pieces. A sharp gouge will leave a smooth surface in the finger pull, so you shouldn't have to sand down in. Try not to oversand the bevels or the top may become too loose in the grooves.

Nailing the Rabbets

If you clip 3d bright finish nails shorter (to about ⅞ in. long), they'll work fine. If you prefer decorative nails with faceted heads, you can find them at specialty hardware outlets such as Whitechapel Ltd.

1. Mark pilot holes for the nails spaced evenly along the joint and ¼ in. in from the edge. Although I mark for three nails, two or four nails would hold just fine. Take care not to place a nail right above a groove. **A**

2. Make pilot holes using a 3d nail with the head cut off for a drill bit. This technique works well in soft woods and leaves a perfect-size hole. In any case, I've broken most of my small drill bits, so I have to use nails. **B** (below)

A

SPACE EVEN MARKS FOR THE NAIL HOLES along the rabbet edge with a tape measure or ruler.

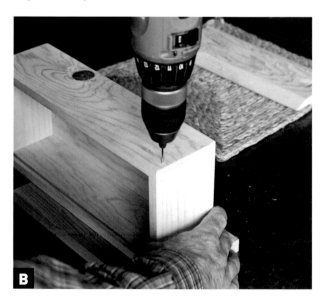

B

DRILL PILOT HOLES FOR THE NAILS using a nail that's been trimmed down for a drill bit.

C

HAMMER THE NAILS INTO THE RABBET flush with the surface. Use a soft piece of pine for a backing board to avoid marring the opposite face.

3. As 3d nails are 1¼ in. long, they are too long for the joints in this box. So clip the ends off, making them about ⅞ in. long. An advantage to this is that cut nails have a blunt tip that is less likely to split the wood.

work SMART

Don't sand out a dent. The flat spot will rise later and produce a bump. Instead, wet the area with a drop or two of water, then touch it with a hot iron. One to three applications will steam out any dent, especially in softwoods.

4. Drive the nails flush with the surface using a small or brad hammer. Then set them with a nailset. Use a backing board of pine if your bench is not perfectly smooth to avoid denting or marring your box. **C**

Finishing

You can leave the box unfinished if you like, but over time the top and edges will get a bit dirty from grubby fingers. A Danish oil and wax finish will also wear over time, but adds luster to the wood.

1. Brush or rub oil evenly on all the exterior surfaces of the box and the top. The pine will soak up the finish very quickly and endlessly, so ignore the directions on the can that recommend replenishing dry areas. **A** Too much oil can even lead to blotching in pine.

2. Apply another even coat in a half hour or so and let it sit for a few minutes.

3. Wipe the surfaces dry if any finish hasn't penetrated. Let the finish cure for a day or two. Rub all the surfaces with a dry cloth to burnish the wood.

4. If you prefer a bit of shine, apply a coat of clear wax.

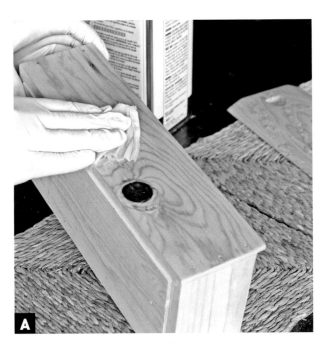

A

APPLY DANISH OIL WITH A BRUSH or rag to all surfaces of the box and the top.

3 Simple Dovetailed Box

In many years of woodworking, I'm not sure if I've found greater satisfaction than with the first dovetailed box I made. Building it, however, was nerve wracking. I puzzled over the angles and spacing. While sawing, I forgot what was waste and what was not. When the joints looked right but didn't go together, I was sorely tempted to reach for a hammer. But was I thrilled when I got the box together in the end.

This is a really simple, unadorned box, and excellent as a first dovetailed project. It's also useful for "male jewelry." I have one on my dresser. It holds a jumble of cuff links, two watches, a miniature compass, three tie tacks, ticket stubs from a 1985 Tom Petty concert, two jackknifes, and a broken ink pen. If you don't need such a box, well, then it also makes a great gift.

The basic design for this box was passed along to me by a fellow woodworker who learned it from another woodworker, and so on, back, I'd guess, all the way to the Egyptians. The top and bottom are captured in grooves. You glue together a sealed box, then saw it into a separate top and case. This approach simplifies the project and ensures the top and bottom halves match.

The surface-mount hinges and cut-in handle greatly simplify the project's details. The one challenge is the dovetails. If you're new to them, cut a practice set or two before you make the box. Then feel the triumph when you put it together and it looks great.

DOVETAILED BOX

Although few woodworkers would call dovetails "simple," this box is as close as you can get. You work with four sides, a top, and a bottom. There are no other parts except the hinges, and they're surface mounted. Only after assembly do you separate top from bottom. The handle is nothing more than a little recess to fit a fingertip. Though minimal, it works. The bottom can be plywood glued into its groove for greater strength. Stopped grooves are necessary, as through dovetails don't hide through grooves.

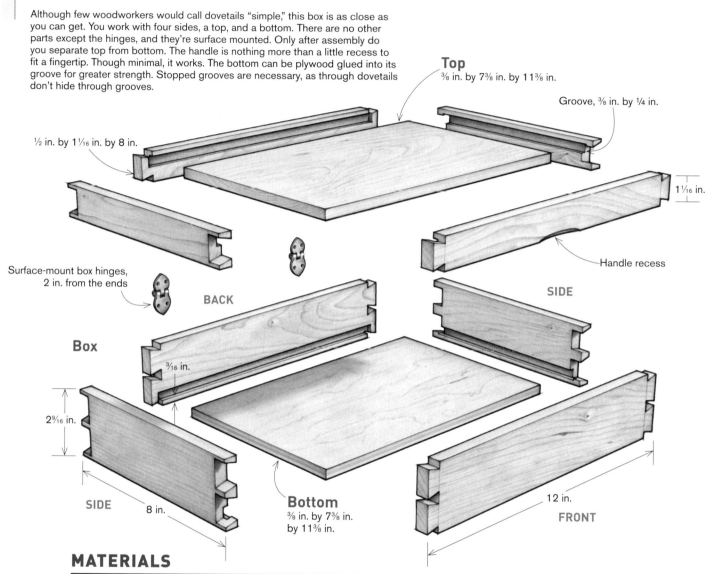

Top
⅜ in. by 7⅜ in. by 11⅜ in.

Groove, ⅜ in. by ¼ in.

½ in. by 1¹⁄₁₆ in. by 8 in.

1¹⁄₁₆ in.

Handle recess

Surface-mount box hinges, 2 in. from the ends

BACK

SIDE

Box

³⁄₁₆ in.

2⁹⁄₁₆ in.

SIDE   8 in.

Bottom
⅜ in. by 7⅜ in. by 11⅜ in.

12 in.

FRONT

MATERIALS

Quantity	Part	Actual Size	Construction Notes
2	Front and Back	½ in. by 3¾ in. by 12 in.	Solid cherry
1	Top	⅜ in. by 7⅜ in. by 11⅜ in.	Solid cherry
2	Sides	½ in. by 3¾ in. by 8 in.	Solid cherry; the sides are half the width of the top, so you can get all your parts from one 8-in -wide board.
1	Bottom	⅜ in. by 7⅜ in. by 11⅜ in.	Cherry plywood
2	Surface mount box hinges	1¾ in. by ¾ in.	Available from Whitechapel, Ltd. Stock number, 247H254A 800-468-5534

Milling the Cherry Stock

Cherry is an easy wood to work. It is medium in hardness, which means it is not a chore to cut with hand tools, yet it doesn't dent or crush easily. The main trouble with cherry is the sapwood, which is a bright cream color that only yellows with age. Sadly, most cherry lumber is sold with a lot of sapwood, making it hard to work around. So at the lumber yard inspect your boards carefully if you wish to avoid a two-toned box.

work SMART

When you don't have what you need, can you make do with what you have? For example, the plans call for two 3¾-in.-wide pieces, but if all you have is a 7½-in.-wide board, feel free to redesign the dimensions of the box. Just make sure the intended contents for your box will still fit.

1. From your rough stock, crosscut oversize blanks, about 13 in. long, for the two sides. Crosscut one 17-in. blank for the two ends because they're too short on their own for milling. And crosscut a blank for the top, also 1 in. oversize. A handsaw and bench hook work fine, but a chop saw is faster. **A**

2. Rip the side pieces to about ¼ in. over width on a tablesaw. **B**

3. Joint a flat face on each board. Plane the sides down to ⅜ in. thickness and the top to ½ in. If you don't have an 8-in. jointer, rip the top into two 4-in.-wide pieces. Mill them with the sides, then glue them back together after you've gotten them to final thickness. Depending on the grain, the joint can be invisible. **C**

CUT YOUR BOX PARTS TO ROUGH, oversize lengths. If you have a long enough board, try to cut around knots and other defects.

RIP YOUR WIDER ROUGH STOCK to ¼-in.-oversize workpieces on the tablesaw. Guard removed for clarity, of course.

JOINT THE FACES FLAT ON A JOINTER. The push block gives a better grip than your bare hands on smooth boards. And it's safer.

D

LET YOUR MILLED BOARDS STAND UPRIGHT overnight in an out-of-the-way place in your shop. This lets them release internal stresses before final milling.

4. Stack the parts on edge in your shop for a day to let any internal stresses show themselves. **D**

5. If the boards have bowed, cupped, or twisted overnight, joint them flat again. Then plane them all to the final ½-in. thickness. Plane the top down to ³⁄₈ in. thickness.

6. Rip the boards to finished width and crosscut them to finished length. **E & F**

E

RIP THE SIDES AND ENDS TO WIDTH on the tablesaw, after milling to final thickness.

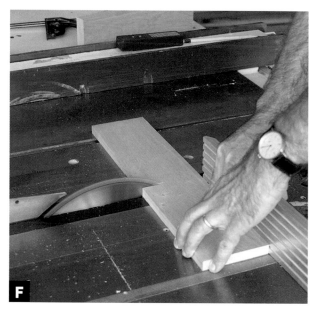

F

CROSSCUT THE FRONT, BACK, AND SIDES to length on the tablesaw.

PLYWOOD OR SOLID

Because the top and bottom of this box are flat and captured on all edges, both can be made from ¼-in. or ³⁄₈-in. plywood. There are several advantages to this. First, plywood is stronger then solid wood and can be glued into its groove (solid wood should never be). Second, plywood is a time saver because it doesn't need as much milling.

The trouble with plywood, however, is that the surface veneers have seams. Although some are nearly invisible, others shrink apart over time and show the lighter-colored core veneers. So in this project, I make a solid top for looks and a plywood bottom for ease and strength.

One big mistake to avoid is using a thin and light ⅛-in.-thick plywood bottom with a thick and heavy solid-wood top. The top-heavy box will fall over backward every time you open it.

SCRIBE A BASELINE ON BOTH FACES of each end of all four side pieces. Set the marking gauge to the thickness of the pieces.

7. For the bottom, you can mill a piece of solid cherry to ³/₈ in. thick, or use a piece of plywood. I used two pieces of ³/₁₆-in. cherry plywood glued together because I had them in the shop. (See "Plywood or Solid" on the facing page for my reasons.)

Planning and Cutting Dovetails

In the dovetailing courses I've taught, most students have found a sample set to pore over very useful. Of course, you need to make that first set to have it to study (it's a chicken and egg thing).

My dovetailing strategies have become habit over the years, both good and bad. I'll show you the whole process, though I admit taking shortcuts sometimes. It's traditional to cut half pins, not half tails. I've also made one tail wider to accommodate the kerf of material lost when the box is sawn in two.

The Tails

1. Set your marking gauge to the thickness of your boards. Scratch your baseline on both faces of each end of all four side pieces. **A**

MARK EACH JOINT WITH MATCHING LETTERS or symbols to keep track of them as you work. Also write "pins" or "tails" on the outside of each piece to avoid confusion.

2. Align the front, back, and sides as you want them in the finished box. Label the joints on the top edge (I use "A-B-C-D" for the four joints). I mark the outside faces with "Tails," and on the sides I write "Pins," to keep track of which way is out and which part of the joint goes on which board. Believe me, all this writing helps avoid disasters. **B**

3. With a marking gauge scratch two parallel lines, ⅛ in. apart, along the faces of all four boards,

C

SCRIBE A DOUBLE LINE ACROSS THE FACE of each board to indicate where you'll cut the top half from the bottom half after assembly.

$1\frac{1}{16}$ in. from the top edge. This marks the kerf where you will saw the box in two after assembly. It's important to mark these lines before you lay out the dovetails because they show the boundary between the top and bottom of the box. **C**

4. On each end of the tail boards, mark lines $\frac{1}{8}$ in. from each end. Then space the tops of the tails evenly, as shown in the drawing below. It's

APPROXIMATE DOVETAIL SPACING

Start with the two $\frac{1}{8}$-in.-wide half pin lines at either end, then divide the remaining space evenly, taking into consideration the kerf you'll lose later. As for errors, the less evenly spaced dovetails are, the more they say "handmade." So give yourself a break if you're not precise.

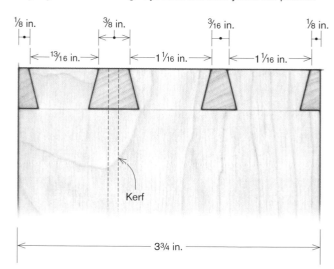

important to space the tails around the kerf farther apart. When you cut the box apart, the resulting half-pins should look like a proper-size whole one.

5. Across the ends of both tail boards, use a square to draw the lines that describe the tails. Then set your T-bevel for the angles of the tails and mark the angles on the face of one board. **D & E** The right angle for dovetails is simple to get. I've never found recommended degrees and such useful. I set my T-bevel off another set of dovetails in my

D

MARK THE TOPS OF THE TAIL BOARDS with a square. Space them according to the drawing at left.

E

WITH A BEVEL GAUGE, MARK THE ANGLES for the tails on the faces of the boards.

PAPER ANGLES

Though they're helpful, you don't need a T-bevel, angle guide, or protractor to lay out good dovetail angles. You can make do with a piece of paper, a pencil, and a ruler.

Measure 1 in. from a corner along the short side of a sheet of paper and make a mark. Measure 6 in. from the same corner but along the long side. Draw a straight line between the two marks and cut along it. You've just made an adequate dovetail jig.

To use it, fold the remaining piece of paper at 90 degrees across its width, then drape it over your workpiece. Mark out your tails as necessary. It's that easy.

shop or by eye. But if you don't have a sample joint or layout jig and are uncomfortable doing it by eye, try the technique in "Paper Angles" above.

6. With a fine-toothed saw, cut your marked lines down to the base line. The toughest part is sawing exactly to your line, so keep your eyes open and pay lots of attention to the way you hold the saw. Sawing two boards at once helps ensure accuracy. **F**

7. Turn the boards sideways in the vise and cut off the waste at the ends. **G** (on p. 38)

SAW THE EDGES OF THE TAILS with a fine-tooth saw, being very careful to stay on the line. Cut both boards at once for better accuracy.

8. In softer woods such as cherry, I chop out the waste between the tails. Your first cut should be well off the baseline, as the chisel will move toward it during the cut. If you start at the baseline, the chisel will dig in past the baseline. Chop from both sides and knock out the chips. A coping saw with a thin blade is another good tool to use for removing the waste between the tails, as is a bandsaw or scrollsaw. **H**

9. For the tails on the other end of the front and back pieces, use the ones you just cut as a template.

The Pins

1. Unlike the tails, you lay out the pins individually using the matched set of tails as a template. This ensures that each joint fits perfectly. So place the "A" tail board over the end of the "A" pin board and trace the tails onto the ends of the pin board with a pencil. **A**

G

CUT THE WASTE OFF THE ENDS of the tail boards, just inside the baselines. Saw both boards at the same time.

A

TRACE THE OUTLINE OF THE TAILS onto the end of the pin board. Do this for each matching pair, being careful that the boards are oriented with their outside faces facing, well, outside.

H

CHOP OUT THE WASTE BETWEEN THE TAILS with a small chisel. Your first cut should be well in from the baseline.

2. With a square, mark straight lines on the face of the pin boards down to the baseline. This is a source of confusion for many woodworkers, because whereas you use a square on the *ends* of the tail boards, you use it on the *faces* of the pin boards. Checking with a complete set of dovetails will remind you which face and which end have straight lines on them. **B**

USING A SQUARE, MARK THE FACES of the pins down to the baseline.

MARK THE WASTE ON THE PIN BOARDS so you don't get confused when sawing.

3. Mark the waste between the pins. This is a key orienting technique. Without those marks it can be very easy to cut out the wrong parts, or simply on the wrong side of your line. **C**

4. Saw just inside of the lines you marked (on the waste side). It's best to leave the pins large. Don't saw directly on your guidelines. **D**

5. Use a wide chisel to chop out the waste so the base line is straight. Of course, you can saw out the waste, too. **E**

6. Pare clean the surfaces you've just chopped with a chisel. If you leave them rough, they'll prevent

SAW JUST TO THE SIDE OF YOUR PENCIL LINE, leaving both the line and a little bit of wood. This ensures your pins won't be too loose.

CHOP THE WASTE BETWEEN THE PINS. You can use a smaller chisel for most of the work (they cut deeper faster). But use a wide chisel when you cut to the baseline for straight results.

PARE FLAT THE BASE OF THE PINS. Any stray bits will keep the joint from coming together completely.

the joint from coming together fully. Never cut shallower than the baseline at the edges, but inside where you don't see it's fine to undercut a bit. **F**

Fitting

1. Do not reach for the hammer. Test fit the joint with hand pressure only (and using the palm of your hand like a hammer will hurt). If the joint doesn't start to go together by hand with some effort, then it's too tight. If the joint goes together the first time perfectly, call the local newspaper, as you've just performed a miracle. **A**

2. Feel for where the fit is too tight. Pare down the faces of the offending pins. **B**

3. If the joint is almost together and you need just a slightly bigger push than your hands can muster, it's OK to reach for a hammer. But don't tell anyone. If the tail board splits, I warned you. **C**

IF A PIN IS TOO WIDE OR ANGLED, pare the surface with a chisel. Keep an eye on your layout lines and try to cut straight down.

TEST FIT THE JOINT WITH HAND PRESSURE ONLY. If you can't push it together by hand, fine tune the joint and try again.

A TIGHT-FITTING JOINT IS THE REWARD of patience and careful work. You should be able to put the joint together with hand pressure only.

WITH A BLOCK PLANE, TRIM ALL THE EDGES flush at the corners. If you get much grain tearout, switch to sanding.

Grooves for Captured Top and Bottom

The simplest way to cut the grooves for the top and bottom is on a tablesaw, as shown in Chapter 2 (p. 22). The only problem is that the ends of table-sawn grooves will show at the ends of the dove-tails. Making a stopped cut, however, is tricky and dangerous on a tablesaw (and I don't recommend experimentation). The best way to groove is with a router table, though it can be done with a handheld router if you're extremely careful.

1. Assemble the box sides (without glue). If the joints are a little loose, secure the box with a band clamp or small clamps.

2. Plane the edges even with one another. The edges are the reference for the router table, so an uneven joint at a corner will show up in the groove. **A**

3. With a ¼-in. or ⅜-in. rabbeting bit set ³/₁₆ in. above the edge of the table, cut the groove on the interior of the top and bottom of the box.

work
SMART

If you just want a plywood bottom or top for your box, it doesn't make sense to buy a whole 4-ft. by 8-ft. sheet. Mail order houses, such as Woodcraft and Rockler, and hobbyist stores sell smaller pieces of plywood, usually 24 in. by 32 in.

ROUT THE GROOVES FOR THE TOP AND BOTTOM on a router table. Mind the direction of the bit to avoid climb cutting.

Grooving while the box is assembled gives each piece stability. Just pay attention to the direction of the bit, so you don't engage a climb cut heavily, which can tear the workpiece from your hands. With a ¼-in. bit, you must make two passes to cut the full ⅜-in. width. **B**

C

CHOP THE ROUNDED ENDS OF THE GROOVES with a small chisel. The router can't get all the way into the corners.

4. This technique leaves rounded grooves in each corner. Take the box apart and chop out the corners with a small chisel. An alternative is to round the corners of the top and bottom. However, I always round too much and little gaps show in the corners of the assembled box. **C**

5. Double-check that the top and bottom fit the groove. If they don't, you have the option of sanding the top and bottom down, or widening the groove.

Assembly

A dry-fit assembly is important. When the glue begins to set is not the time to discover the top is too long. But don't dry fit the top and bottom at the same time: Getting the box apart can be really difficult.

1. Sand both sides of the top and bottom up through 220 grit. Also sand the inside faces of the sides, front, and back. Don't bother sanding the outside faces of these parts, as you'll just have to sand them again after assembly. **A**

2. Dry fit the box with just the top captured to make sure everything goes together as planned. Then do the same with just the bottom captured.

A

BEFORE ASSEMBLY, SAND THE INSIDE FACES of the sides and the front and back pieces, and both sides of the top and bottom to 220 grit.

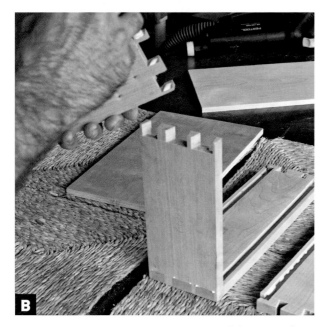

B

APPLY GLUE TO THE FACES OF THE PINS and the groove for the bottom. Try not to get any glue on the edges of the top, as it should float freely in its groove.

C

CLAMP THE BOX TOGETHER. Offset the clamps to get the joint tight despite any tall pins.

3. When you're really sure the box will go together easily, spread glue on the faces of the pins and in between the tails. Spread a little glue in the bottom groove (only if you're using a plywood bottom). **B**

4. Clamp the box together across the faces of the tail boards. The clamps should be slightly offset from the joints. This is because pins can sometimes be a bit too long and will prevent the clamps from bringing the joint together. With this in mind, never clamp so tightly that you distort the shape of the box. If the joints aren't going together at this point, force won't help. Go back to the section on fitting (p. 40). **C**

5. Let the glue cure for at least 24 hours before doing anything else. If you have glue squeeze-out on the inside, use a chisel to cut it out before it hardens.

D

ROUGH SAND THE SIDES OF THE BOX after the glue has set. Don't bother finish sanding until after you've cut the top from the bottom.

6. Rough sand the exterior flat and smooth. You may note some imperfections in your joinery, most probably small gaps. I used to fix these with saw-dust, shims, and glue, but I don't any more unless it's a really big gap and my customer is fussy. Small imperfections are an honest part of the handmade process. **D**

Splitting the Box

You have your choice of how to cut the box apart: large handsaw, bandsaw, or tablesaw. I feel like a magician when I use a handsaw, imagining a trapped assistant inside the box. The bandsaw is faster, but you have to be careful about the blade wandering. I've gotten the best results on the tablesaw, though it's certainly not foolproof.

1. If the grain is plain, mark "front" and "back" on your box on both sides of the cut line. Otherwise it can be hard to tell which way the lid sits after you make the cut.

2. With the blade raised just $^9/_{16}$ in., cut through the two shorter ends first, sawing just between the marks you scribed before you cut the joinery. Try to keep the box flat against the table and firmly against the rip fence.

3. Cut through the long sides last. The fourth cut will free the top. Try to keep either side from wobbling as you cut. **A**

SAW THE BOX IN TWO ON THE TABLESAW, following your scribed lines. Cut the short ends first so your last cut is on a long, more stable side.

4. Plane and sand the edges until top and bottom fit back together seamlessly. This can be a slow process depending on the accuracy of your cut. The plane is better at first because it doesn't round the edges as much as sanders. But if you get tearout, use a sander. **B**

WITH A BLOCK PLANE, smooth the inside edges of the box. Fit the top and bottom so the seam between the two is small and even.

Handle, Hinges, and Finishing

Surface-mount hinges are easy to fit and can be very attractive. They simply screw across the joint. Instead of a handle, I simply cut a recess in the top that allows a finger or two to get hold. It's elegant, minimalist, and it works.

1. Lay out the recess on the edge of the top with a pencil. I made this one about 1/4-in. wide and 2-in. long, but suit yourself. **A**

B

MARK FOR THE SCREW PILOT HOLES with the hinges in place. The pivot pin should be directly over the seam between the top and bottom pieces.

A

MARK GUIDE LINES FOR THE RECESS on the front edge of the top. You don't have to use the recommended measurements if you don't want to.

C

ATTACH THE HINGES TO THE BOX after you've applied the finish. This avoids sticky hinges.

2. Use a file to cut down to your lines. Don't cut all the way in, but at an angle so the seam between top and bottom isn't opened. Sand the recess smooth.

3. For the hinges, clamp the box together and lay the hinges about 2 in. in from the ends. Center the pivot pin over the seam and mark the pilot holes for the screws. Use a drill bit slightly smaller in diameter than the screws. Before you drill the holes, wrap a piece of tape around the drill bit 3/8 in. from the tip to make sure you don't drill through the box. **B**

4. Finish the box with a light coat of Danish oil. If the instructions on the can tell you to replenish dry areas, ignore them. Cherry has a propensity to blotch, even with an oil finish.

5. When the finish dries, screw the hinges in place and you're done. **C**

4 Walnut Display Case

My daughter brings back shells and rocks from every beach we visit. Her room is overflowing with the stuff. They fill her desk and the edges of her bookcase, and line the windowsills. She doesn't see a problem. But the Shaker in me wants a place for everything and everything in its place. So I made this box for her birthday: a nice gift and an unspoken suggestion that she tidy up her room. The plan backfired immediately, as I got a request for enough boxes to store all of her shells. Appreciation is both the woodworker's blessing and curse.

It's a good thing a spline miter is a relatively easy joint to make. Almost all the work is done on a tablesaw with a standard rip fence and miter gauge. Though easy to cut, miters are hard to get just right. If you're a perfectionist and can't stand small gaps, you might find the joint frustrating. On the other hand, lining the bottom is easier than you think. You might end up doing it more often. The trickiest parts are the quadrant hinges. If pressed to make a number of these boxes I might just use the simpler surface mounts from Chapter 3 (p. 45).

In general, display cases allow you to see delicate or valuable things without handling them. Instead of a wood panel in the top, you use glass so the contents are visible when the box is closed. As always, the box should be tailored to its contents. Consider the size and shape of the objects to be displayed, and leave just enough extra space between them and the glass. Arrange the contents on a table and come up with your own dimensions.

WALNUT DISPLAY CASE

This case is a subdued, simple design meant to highlight its contents. Dark, plain-grained walnut generally won't compete for attention with what it is showcasing. However, if you plan to display really dark objects, choose a mild-grained light wood such as birch or maple. The spline miter joints are also unobtrusive. Like the quadrant hinges, they only show when the box is open. Only the laminate nails and hook-and-eye latch show when closed.

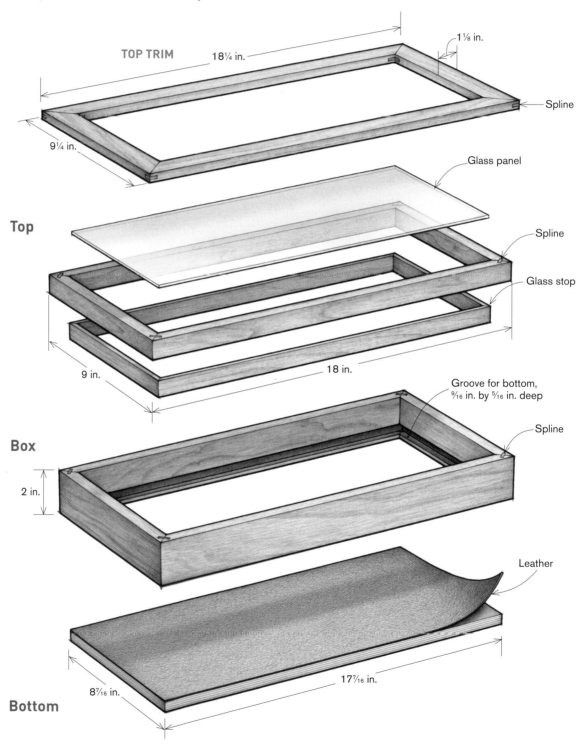

TOP TRIM — 18¼ in.

1⅛ in.

Spline

9¼ in.

Top

Glass panel

Spline

Glass stop

9 in.

18 in.

Groove for bottom, 9⁄16 in. by 5⁄16 in. deep

Spline

Box

2 in.

Leather

8⁷⁄16 in.

17⁷⁄16 in.

Bottom

MATERIALS

Quantity	Part	Actual Size	Construction Notes
2	Box sides	$5/8$ in. by 2 in. by 9 in.	Walnut
2	Box front and back	$5/8$ in. by 2 in. by 18 in.	Walnut
2	Top sides	$5/8$ in. by $7/8$ in. by 9 in.	Walnut
2	Top front and back	$5/8$ in. by $7/8$ in. by 18 in.	Walnut
2	Top trim sides	$3/8$ in. by $1 1/8$ in. by $9 1/4$ in.	Walnut
2	Top trim front and back	$3/8$ in. by $1 1/8$ in. by $18 1/4$ in.	Walnut
1	Bottom	$1/2$ in. by $8 7/16$ in. by $17 7/16$ in.	Plywood
2	Side glass stop	$1/4$ in. by $3/4$ in. by $8 1/2$ in.	Walnut
2	Front and back glass stop	$1/4$ in. by $3/4$ in. by $17 1/2$ in.	Walnut
1 piece	Lining	$8 7/16$ in. by $17 7/16$ in.	Leather or felt
1 pair	Quadrant hinges	$1 1/4$ in. by 1 in. by $1/8$ in.	Available from Brusso®, Inc. Stock number HD-638 212-337-8510
1	Hook and eye	$7/8$ in. by $1/2$ in.	Available from Whitechapel, Ltd. Stock numbers 283HK1, 283HK7 800-468-5534
1	Glass panel	$1/8$ in. by $7 3/4$ in. by $16 3/4$ in.	
12	Brass-plated linoleum nails	$5/8$ in.	

Milling Walnut Stock

Earlier chapters in this book have more detailed information on milling stock to size, and those instructions apply to all the projects in this book. Walnut is medium in density and relatively easy to work. The one challenge is that it's often knotty. Finding straight and clear walnut in good widths can be a challenge.

1. Mill enough walnut for the project to $5/8$ in. thickness, preferably in 5-in. widths and 20-in. lengths. Don't cut short lengths for the sides, but leave them in one 20-in.-long piece.

work
SMART

Pencil lines can be hard to see on dark wood. If this annoys you, try a white artist's pencil and the lines will be hard to miss.

2. Take three 5-in.-wide by 20-in.-long boards. Mark the faces of the three oversize lengths with a large triangle to orient the pieces after you saw them apart. **A** (on p. 50)

A

MARK THE OUTSIDE FACES of your workpieces with triangles. This specific shape makes it easy to keep track of the order and orientation of the parts cut from the board.

B

RIP ONE BOX SIDE, one top side, and one top trim piece from each board to rough width on the tablesaw.

3. From each of the three boards, cut one box side, one top side, and one top trim piece in that order. This ensures the grain matches between the top and sides in the finished box. First rip 2-in.-wide pieces for the box sides from each board, then rip 7/8-in.-wide pieces for the top sides, and finally 1 1/8-in.-wide pieces for the top trim. Save the scrap for making the glass stop later and for test pieces. **B**

4. Plane the top trim pieces to 3/8 in. thickness and set them aside for now.

5. Lay out the pieces according to where they'll be in the final construction and mark the joints on the top edges, the ends, and the faces to keep from losing track of their orientation and jumbling the lot. **C**

C

LABEL THE JOINTS ON THE TOP EDGES after you orient the parts according to how they will go together in the finished box.

SET THE MITER GAUGE exactly 90 degrees from the blade. Use a very accurate square for this job.

TEST YOUR MITER CUTS against a square. Check for gaps inside and outside the joint. If you see the slightest gap, adjust the blade angle accordingly.

work SMART

The small offcuts from mitering with a tilted blade tend to get caught and kicked back. They're harmless unless one catches you in the eye. So wear safety glasses.

Splined Miter

Accurate splined miters are possible on nearly any tablesaw, as long as you take the time to set up the blade and miter fence carefully. You cut the top and bottom sides with the blade tilted at 45 degrees and the miter fence set at 90 degrees square. For the top trim, however, you do the opposite. You cut it with the blade at 90 degrees and the miter gauge at 45 degrees. This is because the spline is vertical in the sides and horizontal in the trim. A rip blade that leaves a flat-bottomed kerf is best for this work, but I'll show you how to work around not having one.

B

Sawing a Miter Accurately

1. Set the tablesaw miter gauge at exactly 90 degrees to the blade. You should see absolutely no gap between blade and square. **A**

2. Tilt the blade to 45 degrees. There's no good way to measure this angle that I know of. Even if there was, I'd still cut a sample joint and check it on a square. Two perfectly cut 45-degree angles should make one tight 90-degree joint. A common problem is the workpiece sliding against the miter fence.

C

ENSURE OPPOSITE PARTS OF THE BOX are the same lengths by using a stop block when cutting the miters. Remember to cut both the top and the box parts with the same setup.

D

CUT THE MITER GROOVE in the ends of each piece ¼-in. deep. A board behind the workpiece can help prevent tearout on the backside of the cut.

E

USE A SMALL CHISEL to flatten the bottom of the spline kerf (if you've used an ATB blade to cut them). Be careful not to deepen the V, just trim it flat.

Some woodworkers go so far as to glue sandpaper to their miter fence, though I think this reduces accuracy. A better solution is making two passes against the blade. The first is off the line. If the workpiece wanders, it's not a problem. Make your second, very light cut the real one. Small engagement with the blade never pushes the workpiece around. **B** (on p. 51)

3. When you have the tablesaw's setup tuned just right, miter one end of the box side and top side pieces (but not the top trim). Cut the miters in the same place on each matched pair, so the triangles on the faces still line up after mitering.

4. Using a stop block to ensure opposite parts are identical lengths, miter the opposite ends of all the box side and top side pieces. **C**

5. Move your miter gauge to the other side of the saw. Clamp a backing board to the miter gauge that will support the workpiece fully in the cut. Set up a stop block opposite the blade. Using test pieces, find the right combination of stop block location and blade height to cut a ¼-in.-deep kerf in the faces of your mitered parts. Locate the kerf about ³⁄₁₆ in. from the inside corner. **D**

6. If you use an ATB blade, your kerfs will have a V-shaped bottom. Use a small chisel to flatten the bottom, cutting from both ends. Be very careful not to deepen the kerf, just trim the V flat. **E**

A

B

CUT A DEEP KERF into a large scrap board with the rip fence set ⅛ in. from the blade. Be cautious where the blade exits the board at the end of the cut.

SEPARATE THE ⅛-IN.-THICK SPLINE STOCK from the larger board with a shallow rip cut.

Make Splines

1. If you can, plane 2-in.-wide stock to just slightly thicker than the thickness of your sawblade, which on my saw is just under ⅛ in. My planer doesn't plane that thin, so I cut spline stock on the tablesaw by ripping on edge, then cutting away the piece. **A & B**

2. Test the spline stock in the kerf. If it's too thick, sand until it just fits. **C**

3. Crosscut splines from the stock on the tablesaw. For consistency and safety, set a block against the rip fence behind the blade. Register the spline stock against the block before each cut. Cut this way, the splines themselves are weak, with the grain running across their width. But the grain is the right direction to give strength across the joint. **D**

C

TEST FIT THE SPLINE STOCK in the miter kerf. You want a tight fit you can press together by hand.

CUT THE SPLINES TO WIDTH on the tablesaw. For accuracy and safety, use a stop block offset from the rip fence so the offcuts aren't kicked back by the blade.

D

LINING A BOX

Bare wood isn't always the best material for the inside of a display case. The grain may distract the eye and some metals will rust when sitting on wood over long periods. Other woods can stain fabrics or impart smells. My dresser drawers still have paper-lined bottoms. So there are very good reasons to line boxes, even if the interior isn't on display.

Boxes can be lined with a huge variety of materials, so don't necessarily reach for felt or leather thinking they are the only options you have.

Thick veneer (1/8 in.) is a great option aesthetically, but leaves you with the same problems that lining is meant to solve. Paper is certainly the cheapest lining, but it doesn't have to look cheap—handmade, acid-free paper can make a very practical and beautiful lining.

Among cloth, you need only consider the thickness. Felt and velvet are most common in part because they're thick enough that adhesives won't bleed through.

LEATHER IS ON THE LEFT, felts and velvet at the top right, shop-sawn cherry veneers in the lower-right corner, and handmade paper in the middle.

Leather-lined boxes are by far the nicest, in my opinion. Although leather costs more, it has a wonderful feel. Leather can be a bit harder to find than fabrics. Local suppliers will be in the yellow pages, but they may insist on full or half-hide minimums, which is a lot of leather and too much for one box. But ask about old samples or a scrap bin. With a little digging, I've found just what I need for a bargain price.

Lining the Bottom

Lining this box is optional and depends largely on what you put in it and how you want the interior to look. I picked a dark green leather as I think it goes well with the dark brown of the walnut.

1. Pick a color for the lining that complements the objects you mean to display and goes well with the wood you use. Get a piece of material that is slightly larger than the box bottom.

2. Measure the thickness of the box bottom and the leather combined, just under $^9/_{16}$ in. in my case. **A**

MEASURE THE TOTAL THICKNESS of the box bottom and the leather lining. Use this measurement for cutting the grooves in the box sides.

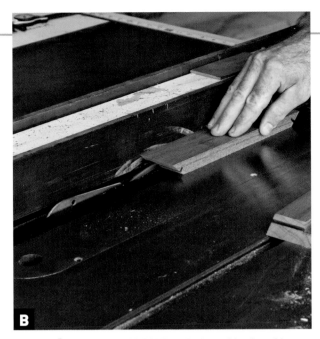

B

CUT THE ⁵/₁₆-IN.-DEEP GROOVE in the box sides by taking multiple passes with a regular blade or fewer passes with a dado blade.

C

CUT A PIECE OF LEATHER slightly larger than the box bottom. You need about ¼ in. to fold over each edge.

3. Rip ⁵/₁₆-in.-deep grooves in the box sides to capture the lined bottom. Make multiple passes with a standard ⅛-in.-wide blade, or use a dado blade if you have one. Test fit the bottom with a piece of the leather and adjust the width of the groove as necessary. **B**

4. Measure from the insides of the grooves and cut the box bottom to size. It should be slightly undersize, ¹/₁₆ in. shorter in both directions, because the leather wraps over the edges and contributes to the length and width.

5. Cut the leather piece just bigger than the bottom, about ½ in. wider and longer. **C**

6. Cut notches at each corner so the leather doesn't overlap when you fold it over the edges. **D**

D

NOTCH EACH CORNER OF THE LEATHER. This will prevent the leather from overlapping when pulled over the edges of the box bottom.

SPREAD A THIN LAYER of white glue evenly across the box bottom. Then lay down the leather. The glue tacks quickly, so try to position the leather accurately the first time.

GENTLY FLATTEN AND SMOOTH the leather against the bottom board with a roller or your bare hands. You don't need to press too hard, just smooth out any lumps.

7. Brush the back side of the leather thoroughly to get rid of any wood chips or dust it might have picked up around your shop. Lightly sand both sides of the plywood bottom piece, too. This step helps avoid a lumpy leather surface.

8. Spread a thin layer of white glue over one side of the bottom piece. **E** Lay the leather down on top and smooth it out with your hands or a roller. You don't need to press hard at all, just smooth out any bumps. **F** There's no need to clamp the leather down.

9. After an hour or two to let the glue set, glue the leather on the edges as well. I use clamps and cauls for this, as leather has some stiffness and may pull away before the glue sets.

Assembling the Box and Top

Although the box and top parts could be made as one and then sawn apart as in Chapter 3, I didn't do that here. I cut the parts separately and assembled them separately. It takes a little longer, but is a bit safer with such a large box. I'm not keen on balancing the small ends on my tablesaw, or creating a large jig to steady the whole box.

1. Sand the inside faces of all the parts. **A**

2. Apply finish to the insides of the box sides with a little Danish oil. You need to finish them first because it's easier to do it now rather than after assembly, when you'd have to mask the leather bottom. **B**

3. Dry fit the box together to make sure the miter joints meet just so. If they don't, your splines could be too long, or the bottom too big. Troubleshoot and adjust as necessary. **C**

A

SAND THE INSIDE FACES of all pieces to 220 grit before assembly. It is far easier to sand them now than when the box is assembled.

B

APPLY A COAT OR TWO of Danish oil to the inside faces of the box parts. Finishing the interior after assembly can stain the leather.

DRY FIT THE BOX with the bottom captured and check that all corners come together accurately. Now is the time to troubleshoot, not when the glue is setting on the splines.

C

INSERT SPLINES IN THE KERFS above the bottom groove. Tap with a hammer to ensure they seat on the bottom of the kerf.

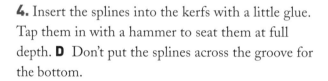

4. Insert the splines into the kerfs with a little glue. Tap them in with a hammer to seat them at full depth. **D** Don't put the splines across the groove for the bottom.

5. Spread glue across the faces of each joint and into the kerfs, and clamp the box sides around the bottom. Clamp from both directions and look to see that the miters come together neatly. **E**

6. For the top, follow the same process as for the box, without finishing the inside faces or capturing a panel. But do check the diagonal measurements after you've applied clamps. Because the parts are thin, they can distort and bend easily. Clamping pressure should bring the joints together without bowing the sides unnecessarily. **F**

CLAMP THE BOX from both directions at each corner. Inspect each joint to ensure that it comes together without a gap.

MEASURE THE DIAGONALS of the top frame to check that you've got a rectangle and not a parallelogram.

Making the Top Trim

The top trim can seem an unnecessary part. After all, why not capture the glass the same way the top was captured in the dovetailed box project in Chapter 3? Wood panels on boxes rarely break, but glass is fragile. You need to build this box so you can take the glass out and put a new piece in. The top trim is a simple way to achieve this.

Like the rest of the box, the trim uses a spline miter at each corner. However, the profile of the trim is such that the kerfing work is done very differently.

1. Mill the top trim pieces you set aside at the start of the project to 3/8 in. thickness.

2. Set your tablesaw's blade to a perfect 90 degrees and the miter fence to 45 degrees. Make test cuts and adjust the miter fence until you get a perfect miter joint. **A**

3. When you cut the miters, stack the pieces that should be the same length and cut them at the same time. With small pieces, this is just as good as using a stop block. Of course, make sure their ends are aligned. **B**

4. To kerf the miters, you need to make a simple jig that holds the workpiece securely, as shown in "Kerfing Jig" on p. 60. I don't recommend trying to kerf the trim by holding it against the rip fence.

5. Set the rip fence so that the kerf cut is exactly centered on the trim pieces. Make test cuts on scrap to get it as close to center as you can. If the kerf isn't centered, the joints between the pieces won't be even. Kerf all four pieces. **C**

CUT THE TOP PARTS two at a time so they're exactly the same length. They're small enough to stack against the miter fence without being unwieldy.

USE A SIMPLE JIG to support the trim pieces while you kerf the ends.

CHECK THE TEST MITER CUTS for the top trim pieces carefully. They'll be very visible in the finished box.

KERFING JIG

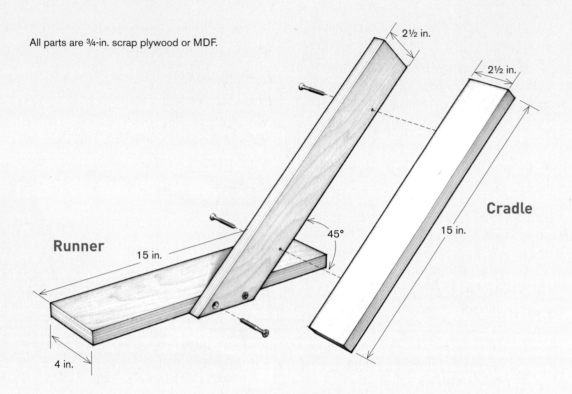

All parts are ¾-in. scrap plywood or MDF.

2½ in.

2½ in.

Cradle

15 in.

45°

Runner

15 in.

4 in.

The jig was built from scrap for this particular box. Unless I plan to make the same box again in the near future, I toss the jig in the scrap bin immediately after use. If I didn't do this, my shop would become overwhelmed with simple jigs.

The main purposes of jigs are to ensure safety and accuracy. This simple one serves both. The risk of a kickback is high trying to kerf the end of a board on a tablesaw without a jig. And even if you avoid disaster, the cut may not be very straight.

The cradle supports the workpiece. The high side makes it easy to clamp the workpiece securely. The runner gives the cradle stability against the rip fence during the cut. The size of the jig gives you plenty of places to hold that are far from the sawblade.

THE WIDTH OF THE SPLINES in the top trim joints should be tight without holding the miter joint apart. Test them before assembly.

6. Crosscut more splines to the exact width of the joint and test them. The splines should be long enough to stick out at both ends. **D**

7. Apply glue to all joint surfaces and clamp the top trim frame together.

8. When the glue dries, trim the overlong splines. This is harder than it sounds, because you need to be careful of the grain direction to avoid chipping out bits of spline. I clamp the frame to a bench top or in a vise and use a chisel on the outside and a fine-toothed saw (not a backsaw) on the inside. **E & F**

9. Sand all surfaces of the top trim to 220 grit.

PARE OFF THE ENDS of the overlong splines with a chisel, remembering to cut with the grain or you may break part of the spline out of the kerf.

SAW THE INTERIOR SPLINE excess flush with the trim frame. You can't use a chisel because you'd have to pare against the grain.

CLAMP THE TOP TRIM and top sides together with even pressure across all parts. Lots of clamps or cauls are necessary.

10. Glue and clamp the box top assembly and the top trim frame together. The trim should overhang the box by about ⅛ in. on all sides. **G**

Setting Quadrant Hinges

Every time I set quadrant hinges, I'm reminded of how difficult they are to fit and swear to use another hinge the next time. However, quadrant hinges are perfect for holding a heavy top open at just past 90 degrees. And they look great. So I used them here, grumbling all the way. If you have a laminate trimmer and the template specific to the hinge (sold by Brusso), then use them as they simplify the process. But I'll show you how to set them with less-specialized tools.

1. Center the forward arm of the hinge on the box side and mark where the screw holes should be. Finish fitting one hinge side at a time to reduce confusion. Don't work on the opposite side of either

hinge until you've finished both mortises in the box side. This strategy will help with correct alignment. **A**

2. Drill pilot holes about ¼ in. deep for all three of the hinge's screws.

MARK THE LOCATIONS for the hinge screws with a pencil. Be sure the hinge is aligned properly, with the pivot point just clear of the box back and the forward arm centered on the side.

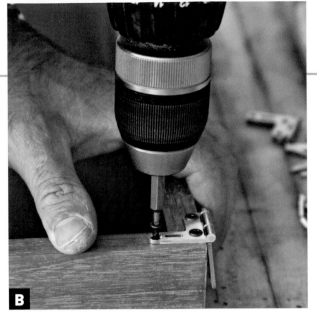

B

ATTACH THE HINGE with steel screws. The screws should be smaller than the finish brass screws.

C

OUTLINE THE HINGE with a sharp pencil. Be as accurate as you can.

D

CHOP OUT THE WASTE right up to your layout lines with a chisel.

E

USE A SMALL GOUGE to cut the curved portions of the hinge mortise.

3. Attach the hinge with steel screws. You don't want to use the brass screws that come with the hinges because you have to take the hinges off and put them back several times. Repeated use of the brass screws will burr their heads. Use steel screws that are shorter than the finish brass screws. This will ensure the brass screws get a good grip. **B**

4. Outline the hinge on the box with a sharp pencil. **C**

5. Set the marking gauge to the thickness of the hinge. Scribe a line along the face of the box to indicate the depth of your cut.

6. Chop the waste out with a chisel right to (but not over) the marking gauge line.

7. Pare the rest of the waste up to your lines with a chisel. Use a small gouge to cut in the curved ends. Be as accurate as you can cutting to your line, trying the hinge occasionally for a good fit. Be careful at the corners of the mortise, as bits can easily flake away. (If they do, try to save them and glue them back after you've finished fitting the hinge). **D & E**

8. Follow the same steps for the hinge on the opposite side of the box.

TRANSFER THE HINGE LOCATIONS to the top of the box. Lay the top of the box on the bottom so they align just so before you mark.

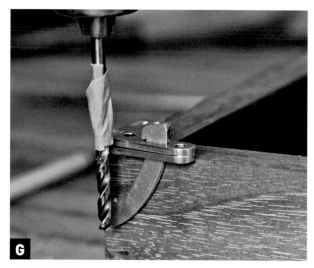

WRAP A PIECE OF TAPE around the drill bit to ensure you cut the quadrant arm mortise at the right depth.

TEST THE QUADRANT ARM mortise depth and shape by placing the hinge in position. This also gives you an idea of the depth and shape of the mortise necessary in the top of the box.

9. Set the top evenly on the box and transfer the hinge locations. **F**

10. Set the hinges in the top as you did for the box.

11. The quadrant arm needs a hole drilled down into the body of the box (and up in the top, though not nearly as deep). With the hinge in place, mark the location of the slot for the arm with a pencil.

12. Use tape to set the drilling depth necessary for the quadrant arm. **G**

13. Drill out a hole wide and deep enough that the quadrant fits down into the box easily. Be careful not to drill too close to the hinge screw holes. **H**

14. Cut up into the box top for the part of the hinge that rests there using the same approach used for the bottom. However, don't drill as deep, just the necessary amount to allow the top of the quadrant arm to fit up into the box top.

15. With the steel screws, set the hinges in place. If you're lucky, everything works smoothly. If not, troubleshoot the problem and adjust accordingly. The most common problem I have is when the holes for the quadrant arm are too small or not in just the right place, the box will not close properly.

Fitting the Glass and Finishing Up

An alternative to the brass-plated linoleum nails that will keep the glass stop in place are brass screws. They take more time to put in, but you're not swinging a hammer near a piece of glass.

1. Mill four pieces of glass stop about ¼ in. thick by ¾ in. wide.

2. Miter the ends on the tablesaw using the top itself to determine exact lengths for each piece. It's best to make miter cuts on small pieces with the miter fence aimed back toward the blade, rather than up toward it in the line of cut. I'm not exactly sure why, but I have a tendency to shatter the tips when I try it that way. **A & B**

3. Sand the inside faces and one edge of each piece of glass stop. The back sides will be hidden, so there's no need to make them look nice.

4. Before finishing, sand all the box parts again with 220 grit to smooth away any scratches gotten while mortising the hinges. Also break the edges (which means to make them less sharp) inside and out by lightly running 220-grit sandpaper over them. **C**

MEASURE THE LENGTH of each piece of glass stop in place against the box top to ensure a good fit.

GIVE THE WHOLE BOX a light sanding with 220-grit paper before finishing. This will remove any light scratches picked up while mortising for the hinges.

CUT THE GLASS STOP MITERS on the tablesaw with a trailing cut. If you angle the miter gauge the other way, the small stop pieces will likely splinter.

work SMART

When ordering glass, subtract at least ⅛ in. from each dimension of the actual recess. Glass cutters are rarely exact, and the glass simply won't fit if it's too big.

APPLY A COAT OR TWO of Danish oil to all parts, being careful not to get any on the leather lining.

5. Apply a coat or two of Danish oil to all parts. Again, avoid getting finish on the leather lining. Let the finish dry before continuing to work on the box. **D**

6. Drill two or three pilot holes in each piece of glass stop, evenly spaced, to secure it in the top. Make the holes the same size or just smaller than the diameter of the nails.

7. Set the glass inside the top and press the glass stop in place. The glass should fit inside the top loosely.

8. Tap the brass-plated linoleum nails home with a small hammer. Check to make sure the nails are not longer than the box sides are thick. **E**

LIGHTLY TAP THE LINOLEUM NAILS in place, being very careful not to strike the glass.

CHOOSING FEET

Boxes don't have to sit flat. You can add feet.

The range of options is unlimited, of course, from your own shop-made ideas to commercial wood and metal feet, both historical and contemporary. But instead of showing a huge range of feet ideas, I'd rather ask, what will feet do to the box?

Compare the photo in this sidebar with the photo at the beginning of the chapter. It's the same box, just the feet are different. I've substituted the felt pad feet that lift the box perhaps 1/16 in. off the surface with these English brass feet.

What words come to mind? Nicer? More elegant? Fancier? With the feet, the box seems

presented, perhaps even poised? Or rather, do they make the box look funny or awkward? Do the feet look like they're not really part of the design, just attached unnaturally?

When you try options such as feet, ask yourself similar questions. If you have the patience and money, try a range of feet until one set pleases. Even sketch options first.

I thought the box looked better without the feet. But I was glad to try them on just to see.

KEEP THE SCREWDRIVER as vertical as possible for the screws under the quadrant arm. The arm makes it hard to drive the screws in at the corners of the hinges.

9. With the top and bottom complete, put the hinges back in place. The hardest part is setting the screws in the corner of the hinges. Access to them is partially obstructed by the quadrant arm. So you must put them in at a slight angle. **F**

10. Put little adhesive felt pad feet on the bottom corners of the box. This keeps the box from scratching surfaces and neatly hides the empty miter kerfs. **G**

FELT PAD FEET STUCK on the bottom corners of the box both hide the spline kerfs and keep the box from scratching the surface it rests on.

The Hook Eye

After the hinges, you'll be glad to know the hook eye is pretty simple to install.

1. Set the box on its back. Center the hook on the front of the box.

2. With a pencil, mark where to drill for the hook and the eye, about equal distance from the top and bottom edges. Remember that the hook should meet the center of the eye as it swings, so locate the hole for the eye accordingly. **A**

3. Use a thin metal rod, such as a drill bit or small screwdriver, to help set the eye in place. **B**

4. If the connection isn't quite right, try bending the hook just a little bit.

REST THE HOOK across the seam between box top and bottom, and mark the locations for the hook's screw and eye bolt.

TURN THE SMALL EYEBOLT into its hole using something small and rigid, such as a drill bit.

5 Fumed Oak Humidor

Humidors made of wood offer a tricky design challenge. The interior should maintain a constant 70-percent level of humidity to keep cigars fresh. But in my house, the relative humidity can drop below 40 percent during the driest times of the year. A box that's wet on the inside and dry on the outside is a recipe for severe warping.

To avoid making an exploding humidor, you need to design it in ways that handle contrasting humidity. Plywood and MDF are slightly superior materials because of their dimensional stability, though I've made solid wood humidors that work fine. The real trick, however, is to line the box tightly with Spanish cedar. The lining acts as a box within the box, helping insulate the structural box from the moisture inside. A heavy coat of finish between the two also helps keep it stable.

Aesthetically, you might wonder what kind of traditional design this is. Yes, you caught me out. It's not based in any particular boxmaking tradition. However, the architectural forms are a traditional source of furniture design, so it's still a traditional box in many regards. The cove detail on the top and quarter-round base are age-old classical profiles. I chose red oak with a fumed finish because fumes seemed appropriate for cigars. I think white oak is more beautiful, but it's harder to find in plywood.

Cigars range from about 4¾ in. long to over 9 in. So unless you smoke one and only one type of cigar, there's not much point in sizing the box to a particular cigar's length. This humidor has an interior of 7¾ in. by 14 in., enough to store cigars of many different sizes and shapes. You can make and add dividers as necessary to separate different types.

FUMED OAK HUMIDOR

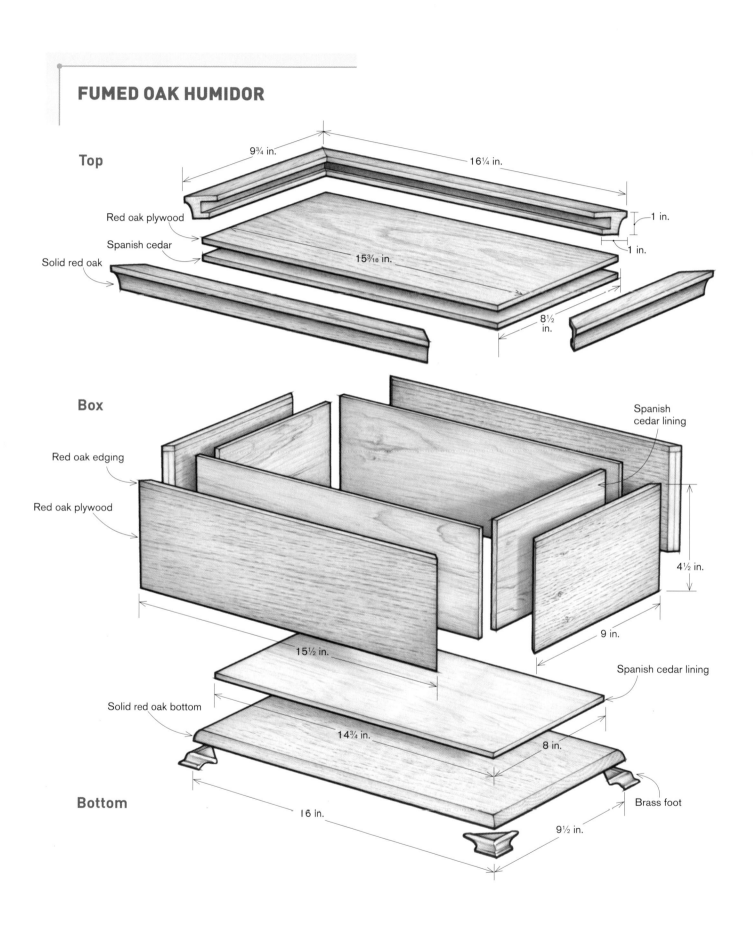

Top

9¾ in.

16¼ in.

Red oak plywood

Spanish cedar

Solid red oak

15³⁄₁₆ in.

1 in.

1 in.

8½ in.

Box

Red oak edging

Red oak plywood

Spanish cedar lining

4½ in.

9 in.

15½ in.

Solid red oak bottom

Spanish cedar lining

14¾ in.

8 in.

Bottom

16 in.

Brass foot

9½ in.

MATERIALS

Quantity	Part	Actual Size	Construction Notes
2	Front and back	15$\frac{1}{2}$ in. by 4$\frac{1}{2}$ in. by $\frac{3}{8}$ in.	$\frac{3}{8}$-in. red oak plywood or two pieces $\frac{3}{16}$ in. plywood
2	Sides	9 in. by 4$\frac{1}{2}$ in. by $\frac{3}{8}$ in.	$\frac{3}{8}$-in. red oak plywood or two pieces $\frac{3}{16}$ in. plywood
1	Bottom	16 in. by 9$\frac{1}{2}$ in. by $\frac{3}{8}$ in.	Solid red oak
1	Top panel	15$\frac{1}{4}$ in. by 8$\frac{3}{4}$ in. by $\frac{3}{16}$ in.	$\frac{3}{16}$-in. red oak plywood
2	Side molding for top	9$\frac{3}{4}$ in. by 1 in. by 1 in.	Solid red oak
2	Front and back molding for top	16$\frac{1}{4}$ in. by 1 in. by 1 in.	Solid red oak
2	Edging for sides	15$\frac{1}{2}$ in. by $\frac{3}{8}$ in. by $\frac{1}{4}$ in.	Solid red oak
2	Edging for sides	9 in. by $\frac{3}{8}$ in. by $\frac{1}{4}$ in.	Solid red oak
2	Front and back lining	14$\frac{3}{4}$ in. by 4$\frac{3}{4}$ in. by $\frac{1}{4}$ in.	Spanish cedar
2	Side lining	7$\frac{5}{8}$ in. by 4$\frac{3}{4}$ in. by $\frac{1}{4}$ in.	Spanish cedar
1	Bottom lining	14$\frac{3}{4}$ in. by 8 in. by $\frac{1}{4}$ in.	Spanish cedar
1	Top lining	15$\frac{1}{4}$ in. by 8$\frac{5}{8}$ in. by $\frac{1}{4}$ in.	Spanish cedar
1	Divider	7$\frac{1}{2}$ in. by 4$\frac{3}{4}$ in. by $\frac{1}{4}$ in.	Spanish cedar
2	90-degree stop hinges	1$\frac{1}{4}$ in. by $\frac{1}{2}$ in. by $\frac{5}{32}$ in.	Available from Brusso, Inc.; Stock number JB 102; 212-337-8510
1	Half mortise lock		Available from Whitechapel, Ltd.; Stock number 76L17; 800-468-5534
4	Feet		Available from Whitechapel, Ltd. Stock number 261VC5
1	Credo Rondo humidifier		Available from BC Specialties, 805-583-8146
1	Credo 55mm analog hygrometer		Available from BC Specialties 805-583-8146

Milling the Parts

I bought one small sheet of $\frac{3}{16}$-in.-thick (nominally $\frac{1}{4}$-in.-thick) plywood for this project. This way I had to glue up pieces for the $\frac{3}{8}$-in.-thick sides and bottom, but I didn't need to buy two separate sheets for the project.

1. Rip pieces of $\frac{3}{16}$-in. plywood 4$\frac{1}{2}$ in. wide, enough for the sides (front and back, too) of the box. Remember that you have to double them up. The tablesaw is the best tool for this job, though I have ripped and crosscut plywood with a handsaw. The trouble is crosscuts get very splintery. Also cut a single piece of $\frac{3}{16}$-in. plywood for the top panel to finished dimensions.

2. Glue the pieces for the sides back to back to make $\frac{3}{8}$-in.-thick blanks. Spread glue evenly on the backs of each piece so the good sides are out.

A

USE FLAT PLYWOOD CAULS and strong clamps when you glue up two pieces of ³/₁₆-in. plywood for the box sides.

C

MAKE SURE YOU ALIGN the solid oak edging perfectly with the box sides. Clamp two at once, with the edging inward, to ensure even pressure along the length.

B

RIP BOTH EDGES OF THE PLYWOOD SIDES on the tablesaw. First, rip one edge over finished width, then rip the opposite edge to final width.

D

CAREFULLY SAND THE EDGING FLUSH with the faces of the sides. Try to angle the sander very slightly away from the face to avoid sanding the veneer. Use pencil marks on the face to guard against this.

Use large pieces of plywood or flat stock as cauls for even clamping pressure. **A**

3. When the glue dries, cut the plywood sides to final width and length. Running plywood over a jointer will dull the blades quickly. It's far better to use only the tablesaw to cut both edges. **B**

4. Mill strips of solid red oak edging, ¹/₄ in. by ³/₈ in. thick (or just thicker than the glued-up sides). Glue them to the edges of the plywood sides, making sure they're centered on the plywood. **C**

5. After the glue has dried, sand the strips flush with the plywood faces. This is slightly tricky because you don't want to sand through the thin plywood faces. I use pencil marks as a guide and hold the sander so it only touches the strips until the edging is flush with the surface. If budget isn't an issue, there are professional tools that do this job superbly, such as the Hoffman® edge-lipping planer. **D**

Solid Wood Parts

You might wonder why the humidor has a solid wood bottom. After all, a plywood bottom would be far more dimensionally stable and resist warping better. I just like the look of the solid wood bottom and haven't had one warp on me yet. I could apply solid wood edging to a piece of plywood for belt-and-suspenders safety, but that's more work.

1. Mill solid oak for the bottom, top frame, and edging. Let the pieces sit overnight to release any stress (though red oak tends to be very well behaved). Then joint and plane them flat and to final thickness and width.

2. If you're not working with a single piece for the bottom, then glue up the parts.

3. Rip and crosscut the bottom to finished size. Cut a quarter-round along the edges on a router table or with a handheld router. You can also leave this step until after assembling the box if you're in a rush to see the box come together. **A**

4. Mill Spanish cedar pieces to ¼ in. thick, enough to line the entire box (see dimensions for cedar pieces in the chart on p. 71).

A

ROUND THE EDGES OF THE BOTTOM board on a router table. Cut the ends of the board first, then the sides for best results.

work SMART

If the cedar starts to weep sap as you work, the best course of action is to take it back to the lumberyard and try to get your money back. Wiping with mineral spirits, baking in an oven, microwaving, shouting: I've found none of these really solve the problem.

WHY SPANISH CEDAR?

Technically speaking, a humidor does not have to be lined with Spanish cedar. But it's the traditional material. Cigar manufacturers have used, and still use, Spanish cedar to pack cigars simply because it's an affordable material and doesn't impart a horrible taste to the cigar. As you buy them in Spanish cedar boxes, it make sense to keep them in Spanish cedar boxes.

The one problem with Spanish cedar is that it can have a nasty sap problem. Boards can weep beads of sap that stick to the cigars. Happily, wood with this problem always has this problem. So check the wood carefully before you buy it (and don't buy it if you find evidence of sap bleeding). If you do end up with a sappy board, just get rid of it. Wiping with acetone will only encourage more sap to rise to the surface.

Assembling the Box

In plywood, I've had great success with simple glued miters. They seem to hold together far better than solid wood, though this isn't a scientific claim at all. If you're uncomfortable with only a glued joint, you can add a spline as in Chapter 4 (see p. 51).

1. Set the blade on your tablesaw to exactly 45 degrees. Set the miter gauge at 90 degrees to the blade as best you can. Take two sample cuts on scrap and check that they make a good 90-degree miter. Adjust the tilt of the blade as necessary.

2. Cut the miters on the ends of the sides. Make sure the sides are exactly equal in length, as the front and back should be. **A**

A

MITER THE ENDS OF THE BOX SIDES on the tablesaw. It's a good idea to make two cuts for each miter, one that removes most of the waste and a second that trims right to your line.

3. To begin assembly, butt the sides and ends together in order (end-side-end-side) on your bench, aligned evenly and without gaps. Stretch blue painter's tape over each joint. Don't forget to put the solid wood edges all on the same side. Don't ask why I recommend checking this, but it's better

B

STRETCH PAINTER'S TAPE OVER each miter joint with the boards butting against each other tightly.

to discover it before you apply glue. Also, you don't have to sand the inside faces of the box because they'll be covered by the cedar lining. **B**

4. Apply waterproof glue to the faces of each joint and fold the box into shape. Apply a fair amount of pressure when pulling the tape across the last joint. Check all the joints at both edges. If there's a gap, stretch the tape tighter until the gap disappears. **C**

C

SECURE THE LAST JOINT with stretched painter's tape. Check each corner for gaps and alignment, and stretch the tape more tightly if necessary.

MEASURE THE DIAGONALS OF THE BOX. If they're equal, you have a rectangle. If not, tighten a clamp across the corners of the longest diagonal to make them equal.

SAND THE OUTSIDE OF THE BOX to 220 grit. Sand up to the corners, but not over them. Otherwise you risk sanding through the veneer.

CHECK THE JOINT BETWEEN BOX and bottom for gaps. Mark the high spots with a pencil to plane or sand, and adjust the fit until it's just right.

5. Check the measurements across the diagonals to ensure you have a rectangle and not a parallelogram. **D** Sand the exterior and top edge when the glue dries. Be very careful not to sand through the veneer at the corners by tilting the sander. Keep it as level as you can. **E**

6. To get a tight seam between the box and the bottom you may need to plane the edge of the box. Place the box on the bottom and check the seam. Mark where the box touches and plane these high spots until the box sits evenly on the bottom. **F**

7. Apply a thin strip of waterproof glue on the edge of the box and clamp it to the bottom. Lots of clamps will ensure even pressure all along the joint. **G**

CLAMP THE BOX TO THE BOTTOM with many clamps, adding a clamp wherever the joint hasn't come together.

GROOVE THE INSIDE FACE of the top molding on the tablesaw. Many passes with a single blade will do the trick.

CUT A COVE ON THE OUTSIDE FACE of the top molding on a router table. Be sure to leave enough wood between the cove and the groove for the molding to be sturdy.

Top Frame and Panel

The top is a mitered frame that uses a plywood panel for much of its strength. The Spanish cedar lining is also captured, but not glued in place.

1. Cut a groove on the inside faces of the top molding that's the exact width of the combined thickness of the top and its inner cedar lining, about $7/16$ in. The groove should be about $1/2$ in. deep and $3/16$ in. from the top face of the molding. You can set up a dado blade for this work or make several passes with the tablesaw blade. **A**

2. Mold the bottom edge with a cove bit on a router table. The key is to leave enough stock between the cove and the groove so the molding

SAND THE COVE WITH A DOWEL wrapped in sandpaper.

doesn't become weak. If you prefer a different profile, by all means experiment and see what you can come up with. **B**

3. Sand the stock smooth. A power sander will work on the flat surfaces, but use a dowel wrapped in sandpaper to smooth the cove. **C**

4. Miter the moldings for the top about $3/4$ in. longer than the box. This way the top will overhang by $3/8$ in. on either side. However, it's most important that the inside faces of the mitered moldings are

work SMART

When laying out parts for the frame, consider the grain and orient the pieces to look their best. I put all the flatsawn faces up, so the sides better match the front of the box.

TRIM ¼ IN. OFF THE INSIDE EDGE of the molding. This cut aligns the molding with the inside face of the box.

exactly as long as the internal dimensions of the box so that the box shuts flush with the lining inside.

5. Rip ¼ in. off the bottom of the molding. This will make the inside edge of the molding even with the inside of the box. If your molding is a different size or shape, then rip the ¼ in. off the bottom of the molding first, then cut the miters so the inside faces line up with the inside edges of the box. **D**

6. Cut the plywood top to fit inside the frame. It shouldn't be so big as to keep the miters apart, but it shouldn't rattle about in the frame. Cut the cedar lining to the same size.

7. Coat the inside face of the plywood top with a clear varnish, polyurethane, or even a thin epoxy. At the same time, coat the inside of the box the same way. The finish will act as a vapor barrier, unseen behind the lining. I used an acid brush because the quality of the finish is unimportant and I don't have to clean a good brush in solvents afterward. Apply several layers of finish and let them cure. **E**

8. When you're ready to assemble everything, add a bead of waterproof glue between the panel and cedar lining. This will help keep the lining centered. **F**

9. Apply waterproof glue inside the top of the groove where the plywood panel will touch it (but not where the cedar lining will). Add glue to the

APPLY A FINISH TO THE INSIDE FACE of the top panel. As the quality of the finish surface is irrelevant, you can afford to use a cheap brush.

RUN A BEAD OF GLUE down the middle of the back of the cedar lining for the top. This will attach it to the plywood panel but let it expand and contract.

CLAMP THE TOP MOLDINGS around the plywood panel and lining. Check the corner joints for alignment and fit, both on the top and below.

miter faces and clamp the top together. Taping around the corners can help with alignment, but isn't enough, as the profile of the molding isn't flat. Check the joints and readjust the clamps as needed so everything lines up as planned. **G**

10. When the glue cures, sand the corners flat if necessary. An alternative technique is to cut the cove after you glue up the frame. This approach makes glue-up easier, but the cove cutting is a little harder.

Fitting the Hinges

I used small stop hinges. Their square knuckle profile makes them stop at about 100 degrees, just past straight up and down. The design of the top precludes the use of surface-mount hinges. And you have to do a little extra work to use the stop hinges.

1. Locate the hinges about 1¼ in. from the ends of the box. With a pencil or knife, scribe the width of the hinge. If you prefer greater accuracy, mark the width and scribe the lines with a square. **A**

2. Set the marking gauge to the width of the hinge (not including the knuckles) and scribe that line on the edge of the box. Then set the gauge to the thickness of the hinge and scribe that line on the face of the box back. **B**

MARK THE LOCATION OF THE HINGES about 1¼ in. from the ends of the box.

B

USE A MARKING GAUGE to scribe the width of the hinge on the box back.

3. You can chop out the waste with a chisel or cut it with a router. Just use the layout lines as your guide. After removing the bulk of the waste, pare the mortises with a chisel to get the fit just right. **C**

4. Rest the top on the box and align it properly. Transfer the hinge mortise locations to the top as carefully as you can.

5. Cutting the hinge mortises in the top is the same as on the box with one big exception. The top is wider than the box, so you can't use the marking gauge to determine the distance of the hinge from the outside edge. Instead, subtract the width of the hinge leaves from the thickness of the box sides (which should be $5/16$ in. from $3/8$ in., so it's $1/16$ in.). To locate the hinges, measure $1/16$ in. from the *inside* edge of the box top. **D**

6. For the knuckles to turn freely, you need to deepen the mortise at the edge. This is because the top edge overhangs and will otherwise interfere with the hinge action.

7. Screw the hinges in place and test them.

C

CUT OUT THE HINGE MORTISE with a straight bit in a laminate trimmer. Keep well away from your layout lines (later pare to them with a chisel).

D

LAY OUT THE BACK OF THE MORTISE on the back edge of the top with a square, measuring $1/16$ in. from the inside edge.

A

MEASURE THE DISTANCE from the post to the top of the lip of the mortise lock. Usually in small locks it's ½ in.

Fitting the Mortise Lock

As we all know, smoking is dangerous, so fitting a lock on this humidor will help keep dangerous cigars out of the hands of friends and relatives. Of course, if you prefer your humidor to be an attractive nuisance, don't bother fitting the lock.

1. Measure the distance from the lock's pin to the top of the lip. On the locks I use, it is ½ in. **A**

2. Drill a ⅛-in. hole in the face of the box, centered and ½ in. from the top edge. The hole helps you orient the lock.

3. Align the lock on the box, centering the pin on the hole from the inside. Mark the edges of the body of the lock (not the plate or lip). Use the marking gauge to lay out the depth of the body. **B**

B

USE A MARKING GAUGE to scribe a line that describes the depth of the lock's body in the box front. Scribe from the inside of the box.

C

SAW THE EDGES OF THE MORTISE for the lock's body. The kerfs won't be very deep, but they're still useful to guide the chisel when you cut out the rest of the waste.

D

CHOP OUT THE WASTE for the lock body from the edge down. Take small bites of the solid oak.

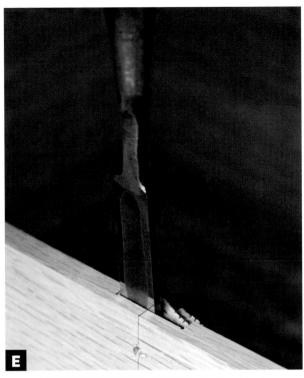

E

PARE OUT THE CHIPS IN THE MORTISE with the chisel oriented parallel to the face.

4. Make angled kerfs on your layout lines with a fine-toothed handsaw inside the box. These kerfs will help prevent tearout when you chop out the waste. **C**

5. Chop out the waste with a chisel. First make small cuts along the top edge in the solid oak. Then clear these chips and gradually cut the mortise down to the layout lines. You'll find it difficult to chop from the inside of the box unless you have cranked chisels and a small hammer (I don't). **D & E**

6. Set the body of the lock into the mortise. You should be able to see the pin centered (though too high) through the ⅛-in. hole you drilled. With a pencil or a knife, mark the ends of the lip on the top edge of the box front. **F**

7. Set a marking gauge to the width of the lip and scratch that line from the inside of the box on the top edge of the side between the lip ends.

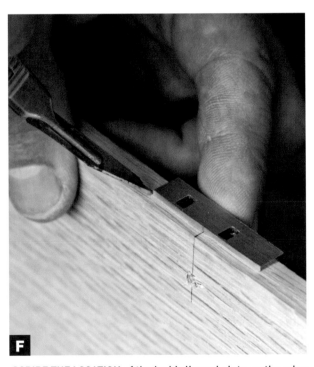

F

SCRIBE THE LOCATION of the lock's lip and plate on the edge and inner face of the box once the body fits in the mortise. Use a knife or sharp pencil for this work.

PARE THE SHALLOW MORTISES for the lip and plate with a sharp chisel.

8. On the inside of the box, scratch the outline of the base of the plate.

9. Chop out and pare a shallow mortise for the lip and plate. This work takes some skill, so go slowly and take off a little at a time. You'll know you're done when the lock fits neatly flush with the top edge and inside face of the box. **G**

Fit the Top Plate

You should fit the top plate after finishing and lining the box with Spanish cedar. But here's how to do it anyway so all the mortise lock fitting information is in one place.

1. Put the plate into the lock mechanism as if the box were locked. Swing the top down on its hinges and press the edge of the top against the plate. There are two protruding knobs that should make dents in the top lid. Remove the top from the box. **A**

2. Drill shallow holes where the knobs made dents in the top edge. The holes should be the same size as the knobs. This will allow the plate to sit flat.

3. Hold the plate in place and outline it with a knife or pencil.

4. Chop a shallow mortise and fit the plate into the top. The fit of the plate determines how well the box closes. It's easier to adjust the plate and hinges' location than the lock's position. Also remember the brass knobs of the plate can be filed for fine adjustment of the mechanism. **B**

A

PRESS THE LID DOWN on the upper plate (fitted in the lock). The fingers on the plate will dent the underside of the top and mark the location where you should mortise for the plate.

B

CHOP OUT THE UPPER PLATE MORTISE to an even depth. The depth and alignment of the plate determine how well the box closes, so cut carefully.

PRESS THE ESCUTCHEON IN PLACE over the keyhole and scribe its outline with a sharp pencil.

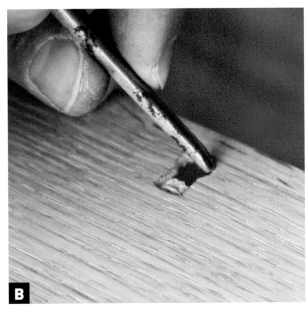

PARE TO YOUR LAYOUT LINE with a gouge and chisel. Cut deep enough for the escutcheon to fit flush with the face of the box.

Fit the Escutcheon

1. Center the escutcheon on the keyhole and draw the outline. **A**

2. With a #8 gouge and a small chisel, pare to the layout lines as exactly as you can. Test the escutcheon in the hole until you can press it into place. If you get a tight fit, you may not need to glue it, but I use a dab of epoxy just in case. Use very little adhesive, as you don't want epoxy running into the lock mechanism. The escutcheon I used had an antique finish, which I made bright by sanding with 400-grit sandpaper to match the humidor's feet. **B & C**

TRY PRESSING THE ESCUTCHEON in place as your cuts near the layout line. You don't want to cut too big a hole, as escutcheons require a tight fit.

TAPE PLASTIC SHEETING over the cedar lining on the inside of the top to give it some protection from the ammonia fumes. Try not to tape over any oak.

SLIDE A SHALLOW DISH OF AMMONIA into your fuming box and close it up. Try not to splash any on the box.

Fuming the Box

Fuming oak with ammonia can make a great finish. When complemented with an oil, you get the most lovely brown tones. It's a relatively simple, though stinky, process. Fuming works with any wood that has tannins. Oak works best because of its high tannin content.

1. Find a cardboard box and plastic bag big enough to fit the box and lid in without touching the sides. Set up a platform with a space for a dish underneath. The platform should be narrow strips of wood so relatively little area of the box and lid rest on it. Triangular slats are best.

2. Mask off the Spanish cedar lining with tape and plastic. You don't really want to fume the cedar if you can help it. **A**

3. Set the box and lid on the platform in the box.

4. Pour about two cups of household ammonia into the dish and slide it into the cardboard box (without splashing the humidor). Close up the box, put the plastic bag over it, and let it sit. How

long? The longer you let the box fume, the darker it will get. Household ammonia is a very weak concentration, so let it sit at least overnight for a light brown finish. For a darker finish, keep replenishing the ammonia over a few days. I don't recommend fuming with industrial-strength ammonia unless you're industrially strong. It's very nasty, corrosive stuff and requires a special breathing apparatus to handle. The household stuff works just the same, it just takes much longer. **B**

5. If the box looks a sickly shade of grayish green when you pull it out, don't panic. That's the way it should look before applying oil.

work
SMART

Before fuming, wipe down the box with mineral spirits. This is an excellent way to find any dried glue squeeze-out. Make sure to sand it off before fuming, as ammonia fumes have a difficult time getting under glue, leaving an uneven finish.

Lining the Box with Spanish Cedar

Building the box within the box will take no time. It just requires some careful crosscutting. Set the mortise lock, but not the hinges, back in place before you line the box.

1. Rip and crosscut a piece for the bottom of the box. It should fit snug end to end, but have perhaps ⅛ in. of play in width.

2. When inserted, the sides of the lining should stand ¼ in. taller than the edge of the box. They should be 4¾ in. wide, but measure your own box and rip accordingly.

3. Trim and insert the long sides first. Dab a line of glue along the center of the inside faces and clamp them to the box sides. This helps prevent the lining from bowing in. **A**

4. Trim and fit the lining ends. Glue them in the same way, with just a small dab.

5. After the glue dries, lightly chamfer the outside edges of the lining. Without this, the box may not close without considerable effort. **B**

A BEAD OF GLUE CENTERED on the back of the lining will keep it in place but let it expand and contract at the edges.

CHAMFER THE OUTSIDE EDGES of the cedar lining. This helps the top close with ease.

HUMIDIFIERS AND HYGROMETERS

Humidors don't work all by themselves. They need a source of moisture and a way to measure it. Hence, you need to fit a humidifier and a hygrometer in your humidor.

The simplest humidifiers are just a piece of specialized foam in a casing. You add water occasionally and the foam releases it in a steady manner. They work fine as long as you remember to add water on a regular basis.

Hygrometers measure relative humidity. Small ones designed for use in a humidor indicate ideal humidity on their scale (a shaded area).

If you're forgetful and budget isn't an issue, there are electronic humidifiers that automatically keep your humidor at ideal levels. They tend to be bulkier and require batteries or a cord plugged into a wall socket.

CLOCKWISE FROM TOP RIGHT: An electronic humidifier with integrated hygrometer and attached battery pack is bulky but convenient; an analog hygrometer with full humidity range indicated; two different styles of foam humidifiers in gold and black.

**THE GLUED FELT ON THE
ENDS** of the dividers
should make a snug, but
not tight, fit.

Moveable Divider and Feet

If you plan to store more than one type of cigar
in your humidor, you shouldn't let them touch. A
moveable divider is an elegant solution.

1. Trim a leftover piece of cedar lining to fit cross-
wise in the box, just a bit loose.

2. With a coping saw or on the bandsaw, cut a
curve out of the top edge, shaped to your eye. I cut
a curve that was about 1 in. lower at the center than
at the ends. It looks better than a straight piece and
suggests it will be easier to get things out of the
box. Finish sand up to 220 grit.

3. With a scissors, cut pieces of felt the same size as
the divider ends that will fit against the sides of the
humidor.

4. Fix the felt on the ends of the divider with yellow glue. The right fit should leave the divider snug
enough to stay put if you move the box around, but
not so tight that it's hard to get the divider into the
box. **A**

5. Attach the feet with screws at each corner. Be
very careful not to use screws longer than the bottom is thick.

 # Shaker Lap Desk

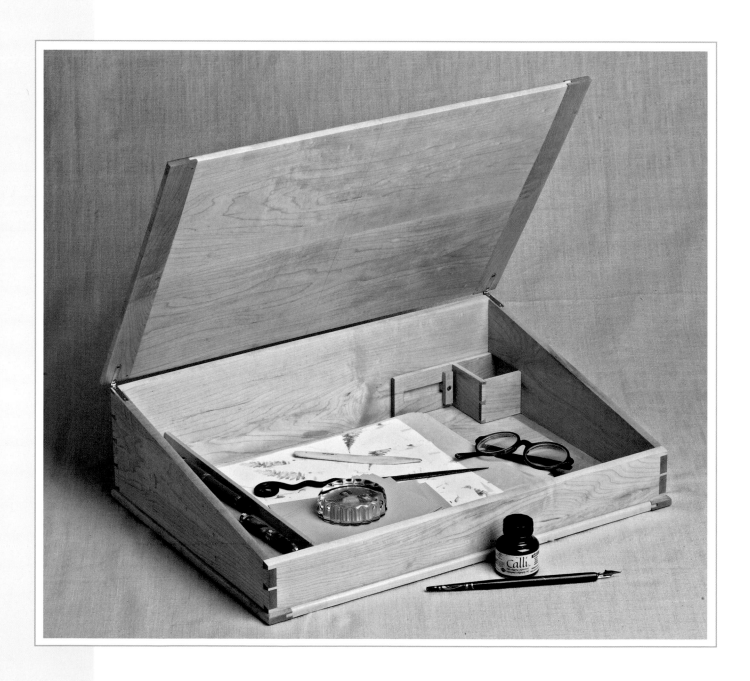

You have to step back in technological history quite a bit before you find lap desks being used. Back to the 19th century, long before the Blackberry®, before the laptop, before the typewriter, to an age when ink pot, pen, and parchment were the stuff of business. So in the early 21st century, you may no longer need a place for paper, pen, and ink pot, but you may need a beautiful box with beautiful details. Hence, this project.

Lap desks stored documents inside. Their tops were smooth writing surfaces, generally angled to make scribbling easier. On the right-hand side was often an ink-pot drawer. The little drawer kept the ink pot at hand, yet nearly impossible to knock over. Some had more than one drawer and other features. A waggish friend suggested the best use for one today is to keep a Blackberry charger, earphones, and other paraphernalia.

I derived this version from the elegant, simple desks built by the Shakers. The Shakers consecrated all their work to God, so they did their very best in all things. And that could be very good indeed. This can translate into jaw-dropping details on their furniture. So, to make this project accessible, I stayed away from the super-fine dovetails and trim. The ink-pot drawer is the hardest part because the dovetails are very small and half-blind. So skip the drawer, if you like, and maybe add a second tray or just let the clean lines stand alone.

Although many of the original desks were made with pine, I chose maple for this one. The light color and iridescence of the wood are most lovely. But it's harder to work with because maple moves as you work it. Sometimes every cut will cause it to bend, bow, or warp anew. Mill slowly and you should be able to avoid the worst problems.

These desks traditionally had a lock to keep nosy people out of important papers. If you'd rather keep your desk simple, skipping the lock is a good strategy. But if you'd like to add a lock, follow the steps provided in Chapter 5 (p. 80).

SHAKER LAP DESK

The writing desk is, at its core, a dovetailed box with slanted sides. Inside, a simple tray for pens fits in a groove. On the other side is a cutout for the ink drawer. The top and bottom panels have breadboard ends to reduce warping over time. Strap hinges connect to the sides, not the box back.

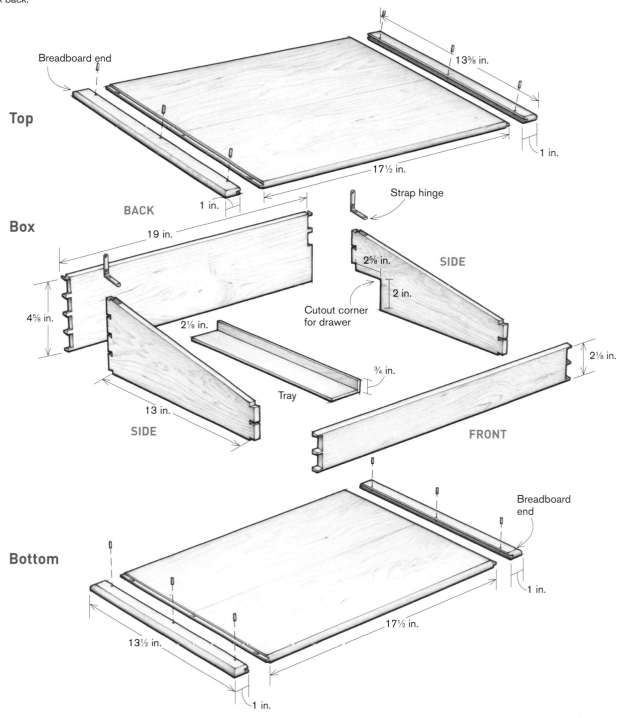

Top

Breadboard end

13⅜ in.

1 in.

17½ in.

BACK

1 in.

Box

19 in.

Strap hinge

SIDE

2⅝ in.

2 in.

Cutout corner for drawer

4⅝ in.

2⅛ in.

13 in.

¾ in.

Tray

2⅛ in.

SIDE

FRONT

Bottom

Breadboard end

1 in.

17½ in.

13½ in.

1 in.

MATERIALS

Quantity	Part	Actual Size	Construction Notes
2	Sides	$\frac{3}{8}$ in. by $4\frac{5}{8}$ in. by 13 in.	Maple
1	Back	$\frac{3}{8}$ in. by $4\frac{5}{8}$ in. by 19 in.	Maple
1	Front	$\frac{3}{8}$ in. by $2\frac{1}{8}$ in. by 19 in.	Maple
2	Panels for top	$\frac{3}{8}$ in. by $6\frac{11}{16}$ in. by $17\frac{1}{2}$ in.	Maple
2	Panels for bottom	$\frac{3}{8}$ in. by $6\frac{3}{4}$ in. by $17\frac{1}{2}$ in.	Maple
2	Breadboard ends for top	$\frac{3}{8}$ in. by 1 in. by $13\frac{3}{8}$ in.	Maple
2	Breadboard ends for bottom	$\frac{3}{8}$ in. by 1 in. by $13\frac{1}{2}$ in.	Maple
1	Tray bottom	$\frac{1}{4}$ in. by $1\frac{7}{8}$ in. by $12\frac{1}{4}$ in.	Maple
1	Tray side	$\frac{1}{4}$ in. by $\frac{3}{4}$ in. by $12\frac{1}{4}$ in.	Maple
1	Drawer front	$\frac{3}{8}$ in. by $2\frac{1}{4}$ in. by $2\frac{7}{8}$ in.	Maple
1	Drawer side	$\frac{1}{4}$ in. by 2 in. by $2\frac{9}{16}$ in.	Maple
1	Long drawer side	$\frac{1}{4}$ in. by 2 in. by $5\frac{1}{2}$ in.	Maple
1	Drawer back	$\frac{1}{4}$ in. by 2 in. by $2\frac{9}{16}$ in.	Maple
1	Drawer bottom	$\frac{1}{4}$ in. by $2\frac{1}{8}$ in. by $2\frac{1}{8}$ in.	Maple
1	T-shaped key	$\frac{3}{8}$ in. by $\frac{1}{2}$ in. by $1\frac{1}{2}$ in.	Maple
1	Knob	$\frac{3}{8}$ in. diameter	Available from Brusso, Inc.; Stock number 102K7A; 212-337-8510
2	Strap hinges	$2\frac{1}{2}$ in. by $\frac{1}{4}$ in.	Available from Whitechapel, Ltd.; Stock number 247HV12; 800-468-5534

Mill the Maple

Original Shaker desks were made from very thin wood, ³⁄₈ in. or less. Their delicacy is beautiful, but it makes the milling process difficult when you start with inch-thick lumber. You can simply grind the boards down with multiple passes through a planer (and if you need garden mulch, this is an excellent option). But I resaw the boards and keep the offcuts for other projects.

1. Write up a full cutting list of all the parts you'll need and their thicknesses (use the materials list on p. 91). Crosscut pieces to length and add a larger

---

RESAWING ON THE TABLESAW

MAKE TWO PASSES over the tablesaw to resaw wide boards.

A HANDSAW AND A LITTLE ELBOW GREASE will finish the cut.

The bandsaw is the best tool for resawing. Because the saw kerf is small, generally less than ¹⁄₁₆ in., you get to keep more solid wood. However, if you don't have a bandsaw, the tablesaw can work well for small pieces. The only disadvantage is that you lose material based on the thickness of the blade, generally ⅛ in.

For wider pieces, however, there are limits to the tablesaw. The height of the blade is generally 3 in. The second issue is power. Full-thickness cuts, especially in harder woods such as maple and oak, will tax the strength of any motor. A sharp blade and slow feed rate help enormously.

Sawing from both sides will double the thickness that you can resaw. For even wider boards, rip from both sides, then saw the remainder in the middle by hand. Though it works perfectly well, it does take some effort (you won't have to go to the gym that day). After a few boards, however, you may find a bandsaw on your shopping list.

CROSSCUT MAPLE BOARDS to rough lengths for every part of the box and a few more. Make piles of related pieces to keep track of what you have.

SCORE A LINE with a marking gauge on the edge of each board ½ in. from the jointed surface.

board or two just in case you mess one up or decide to add a drawer later. I mill everything at once instead of in smaller batches to ensure uniform thickness. And it's more efficient. **A**

2. On the boards, write what part or parts they'll eventually become. It's a good way to keep track of parts and know if you have enough wood for everything.

3. Joint one face and one edge on each board. Then scribe a line ½ in. from the flat surface along the unjointed edge of each board with a marking gauge. This is the line you'll follow when you resaw the boards. **B**

4. Darken the scribe line with a pencil. Even if your eyes aren't as bad as mine, a really distinct line of cut is handy when sawdust blows over the mark during the cut. **C**

5. Resaw the parts on a bandsaw. Run the jointed face against the fence and keep the blade on the far side of your scribe line. You want to end up with two, full ½-in.-thick workpieces. If you don't

DARKEN EACH SCRATCHED LINE with a pencil so you will be able to see it when you resaw the boards.

have a bandsaw, you can resaw the pieces on the tablesaw (see "Resawing on the Tablesaw" on p. 92) or with a handsaw. **D**

6. Stack the parts on edge with airspace between them in an out-of-the-way place for a few days. This gives the internal stresses in the boards time to express themselves and warp the boards before (rather than after) you mill them flat.

7. Joint one face flat on all the boards that need it.

8. Plane all the parts to thickness and hope that your flat stock doesn't continue to warp. **E**

work SMART

Flattening thin stock is hard because the boards are flexible. For example, if you press a bowed board flat on the jointer, each pass will simply make the board thinner without making it flatter. Instead, start cuts in the middle of bowed boards and take small cuts off each end to get rid of bows.

SAW EACH BOARD right on the line, or just outside it, on the bandsaw. Move slowly through the cut to help keep the blade from wandering.

PLANE THE STOCK DOWN to final thickness. Do this only after rough planing the boards and letting them sit to release stress for a few days.

TOO MUCH MOVEMENT IN SERVICE

To improve their profits, sawyers often kiln dry their lumber too fast. This added stress can result in a number of problems, one of which is case hardening. It's easy to spot because the board will pinch the blade as you saw it, creating friction, heat, burning, and sometimes a kickback. This can be a serious problem when resawing on the tablesaw.

What to do? A splitter or riving knife in your tablesaw is essential to help prevent kickbacks. When resawing boards with a lot of internal stress, make many cuts, each ½ in. deeper than the last, rather than one full-thickness cut.

KERFS THAT PINCH TOGETHER are highly dangerous on the tablesaw and indicate case hardening or other internal stresses.

LAY OUT THE ANGLE of the slope on the box sides with a pencil and straightedge.

Shape the Parts

Thankfully, the angled sides of the box don't complicate the joinery. But making two matching, sloped sides takes a trick or two.

1. Joint one edge of each side and rip to width. Then crosscut the front, back, and side pieces to length.

2. Lay out the slope on the sides with a straightedge. **A**

JOINT THE ANGLE on both side pieces at the same time to ensure consistency.

3. Cut the slope on a bandsaw, or by hand with a ripsaw. Stay off your line, because you'll need it in the next step. **B**

4. Holding the two sides together, perfectly aligned end-to-end, joint the sloped edge smooth and to the layout line. You can also clamp them in a bench vise and plane them even with a handplane. **C**

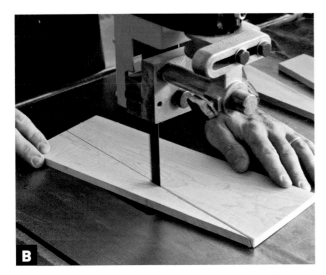

SAW THE ANGLES on a bandsaw. Keep well off your line.

5. Set a T-bevel against the angle of the sides. Transfer the angle to the tablesaw's blade. This is so you can rip the top edges of the front and back to match the slope of the sides. **D & E**

6. Mark where the front intersects the sides. Do the same for the back, then rip the top edges of the front and back on that line on the tablesaw with the blade tilted. **F**

7. Lay out the cutout corner for the drawer in the side piece, which is simple enough. Make the cuts on the tablesaw. Crosscut the vertical line first. Then rip the other side of the cut flat on the tablesaw. Remember the blade cuts farther on the bottom of the board. If you finish the cut while ripping, you'll probably cut past your corner on the underside. So don't complete the cut on the tablesaw, but chop it out with a chisel afterward. **G**

D

WITH A T-BEVEL, measure the angle you cut to transfer it to the tablesaw blade. Take the obtuse, not the acute angle.

F

MARK WHERE THE FRONT and back intersect the sides. On the tablesaw, rip the angle on the front and back pieces.

E

TILT THE BLADE to the angle of the sides using the T-bevel.

G

CROSSCUT THE NOTCH for the ink drawer on the tablesaw. Use the miter fence for the vertical cut.

SCRIBE THE BASELINE for the dovetails on the faces and edges of each board.

CUT THE EDGES of the tails on both front joints at the same time. This will save you a little time and is more accurate.

Dovetail the Main Box

The thinness of the wood means the dovetails will be very small. On the one hand, you'll need good eyesight and a small enough chisel to fit between the tails. On the other hand, thinner wood is easier to cut. Otherwise, there's no substantial difference. For a more detailed step-by-step description of cutting dovetails, see Chapter 3 (p. 35).

1. Scribe the baseline on the edges and faces of each piece. **A**

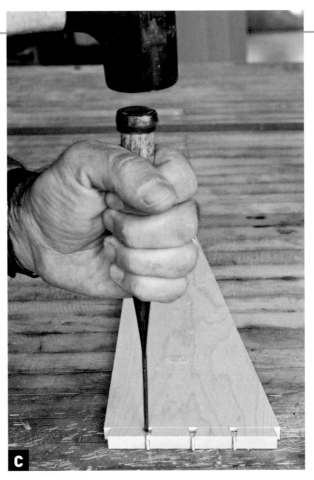

CHOP OUT THE WASTE between tails with a chisel that fits.

2. Lay out the tails on the side pieces. Just ignore the angle and lay out two tails on the front end and four on the back. On the side with the cutout corner, lay out two dovetails.

3. Set your bevel gauge to the desired angle by eye, from another set of dovetails, or by the method shown in Chapter 3 (p. 37). Lay out the sides of the tails.

4. Cut the tails with a backsaw. The set of dovetails at the front of the box should match, so cut the front of both side pieces at the same time. The set at the back do not match, so you'll need to cut them individually. **B**

5. Chop out the waste between the tails. If your smallest chisel is too big to fit between the tails, then you either need to get a smaller chisel or recut your tails farther apart. **C**

CHIP REMOVAL

In the small spaces between tails, it can be devilishly difficult to remove chips. A chisel tends to wedge chips in, not drive them out. Other thin tools around the shop—pencil, screwdriver, fingers—either have the same problems as a chisel or won't fit in the narrow space.

But there are great tools for this: brass punches. They have flat, round faces so they push the chips out rather than wedge them. They also come in sets, so you can chose the right size for the dovetails you're cutting.

USE A BRASS PUNCH with a flat face to dislodge the chips between tails.

6. Use the tails you've cut as a template to lay out the pins for each joint. Because the sides are so thin, you should be able to reach in with a pencil and scribe them easily. Cut out the pins with a backsaw, chop the waste, and fit the joints together. **D**

Yes, that was fast, but use Chapter 3 (p. 35) for the details of this process.

SCRIBE THE TOPS of the pins on the ends of the front and back pieces with a sharp pencil. The thinness of the stock should let you do this without a problem.

Assemble the Main Box and Tray

There aren't any tricks to assembling the main box except the tray. I find it easier to attach it after assembly of the main box, though some work should be done before that stage.

GLUE AND CLAMP the tray side to the bottom. Check that the joint is even at each clamp and that the bottom isn't bowed.

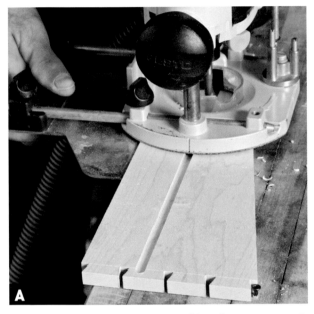

CUT A GROOVE for the interior tray with a plunge router and straight bit. Keep the workpiece from moving by setting screws in the corners of your workbench.

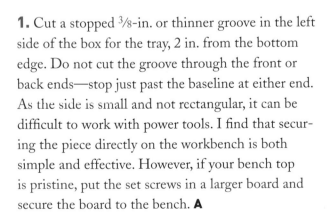

PRESS THE TRAY IN PLACE by hand and check that it's level and straight. A little glue in the groove will secure it in place.

1. Cut a stopped ³⁄₈-in. or thinner groove in the left side of the box for the tray, 2 in. from the bottom edge. Do not cut the groove through the front or back ends—stop just past the baseline at either end. As the side is small and not rectangular, it can be difficult to work with power tools. I find that securing the piece directly on the workbench is both simple and effective. However, if your bench top is pristine, put the set screws in a larger board and secure the board to the bench. **A**

2. Mill the tray stock to the exact width of the groove. Glue the side and bottom of the tray together to make the tray, clamping along the length. Finish-sand the tray after the glue dries. **B**

3. Finish-sand the interior faces of the box sides before assembly. It's always easier to sand flat pieces.

4. Glue and clamp together the four box sides. Use a square to make sure the clamped assembly is rectangular before the glue sets.

5. Measure and trim the tray to fit in the box. Then add a little glue in the groove and press it in place. If it's loose, clamp it until the glue dries. The tray doesn't have and doesn't need any other support. **C**

Breadboard Top and Bottom Panels

Most of the desks I've seen in books and museums have a simple, solid board bottom that's glued or nailed onto the box. I haven't been able to look inside many, but I wonder how many bottoms have split as a consequence of the wide cross-grain joinery. At least all of the tops have breadboard ends. Because I made one for the top, I just went ahead and made another for the bottom. However, please feel free to make a solid board bottom—you'll be just that much more traditional.

1. Glue up the pairs of panels for the top and the bottom. Remember the bottom is slightly wider than the top, otherwise they are identical. You can't use biscuits to align ⅜-in. stock because it's too thin: You'll need to make sure the boards are aligned as you clamp them. This is a simple task of pressing the boards against the clamp bars while you tighten and checking with a finger in case they squirm apart along the seam. Clamp slowly, adjusting with your finger as necessary, and they should align well. **A**

2. Sand off any glue squeeze-out with 100-grit or 120-grit sandpaper. Crosscut the assembled top and bottom to length.

3. Make four breadboard ends 1 in. wide and the same thickness as the top and bottom. These help keep the top panels from cupping over time. However, they can't just be glued on the ends. Seasonal wood movement would break them off. Cut ³/₁₆-in.-wide grooves in them on the tablesaw about ¼ in. deep.

4. Rabbet both sides of the top and bottom panels on a router table with a tall fence. The matching rabbets should be cut just shy of ¼ in. wide and deep enough to allow the resulting tongue to fit snugly in the grooves of the breadboard ends. Alternately, you could use the tablesaw with a tall fence or a shoulder plane. **B**

B

WITH A STRAIGHT BIT in the router table, cut rabbets on both sides of the top and bottom panels. The finished tongue should be exactly the width of the groove in the breadboard ends.

A

AS YOU GLUE UP the top and bottom panels, check that the joints remain aligned and don't slide against one another as you tighten the clamps.

Assembling the Breadboard Ends

Here's the hard part, as you shouldn't just glue the breadboard ends to the panels. Instead, peg the ends in slots so there's free cross-grain movement.

1. Dry-assemble the panels and drill three holes with a 3/32-in. drill bit along the length of the joint. The holes should be about 5/16 in. deep, which is to say as deep as you dare without drilling through. Use tape around the bit as a guide if you like. One hole should be in the middle, the other two about 1 in. from each edge. And the holes should be an equal distance from the edges of the tongue and the groove, about 1/8 in. from the joint. **A**

2. Make square peg stock, 3/32 in. square, on the tablesaw from a larger board. Cut each peg about 5/16 in. long and sharpen one end on a sander or with a chisel. **B**

3. Elongate the holes at either end of the tongue about 1/4 in. To do this, slide the breadboard end a little bit to one side on the panel after drilling the initial holes, about the distance of the diameter of your drill bit. Then use the hole in the breadboard end as a pilot for drilling through the tongue again. Take the breadboard end off and you should find a series of neat holes in the tongue. A little careful chisel or knife work will connect the holes into a slot. **C**

B

RIP 3/32-IN.-SQUARE PEG STOCK from the edge of a larger board on the tablesaw.

C

ELONGATED PEG HOLES at the ends of the tongues allow the panel to move against the breadboard ends without cracking.

A

DRILL 3/32-IN. PEG HOLES about 1 in. from the edge of the panel, centered on the tongue and groove. To avoid drilling through, use blue tape on the drill bit as a depth guide.

SET THE PEGS with a metal hammer against the workbench top. Clamps should hold the end in position. Use a pair of pliers to hold the pegs unless you have really tiny fingers that can't feel pain.

GLUE THE BOTTOM to the box using many clamps to ensure there are no gaps in the seam.

4. Apply glue to the center of the breadboard groove and assemble the panels. With the clamps still in place, hammer the pegs into the holes. **D**

5. After the glue dries, sand the panels flat and smooth. Cut a quarter-round detail on all four sides of both the top and bottom panels with a router bit.

You can do this with either a router and a bearing guided bit, or on a router table with a fence.

6. Finish-sand the top and bottom panels.

7. Simply glue the bottom to the box. Run a bead of glue along the bottom edge of the box sides and center it on the bottom. Add clamps all around. **E**

Make and Install the Ink Drawer

The trickiest part of making this drawer is the small size of the parts. Well, then there's the joinery too. The drawer front is a single piece. It's connected to the sides with stepped half-blind dovetails. If the joinery looks too tricky, skip it and use rabbets or butt joints. They'll work fine for such a small piece and they look great too.

1. Mill a long piece of $3/16$-in.-thick stock for the drawer sides and bottom. Rip it to $2\frac{1}{8}$ in. wide for now.

2. Crosscut one piece $2\frac{1}{8}$ in. long from the end of the long board for the drawer bottom.

3. Rip what remains of the long piece to 2 in. wide, the same dimension as the height of the cutout hole in the right side of the box.

INK DRAWER

The ink drawer is a complex and graceful addition to the lap desk. It uses three types of joints—a regular dovetail, a stepped half-blind dovetail, and a mortise and tenon. The T-shaped key acts both as a stay and a glide for the drawer. It's not meant to turn and let the drawer out.

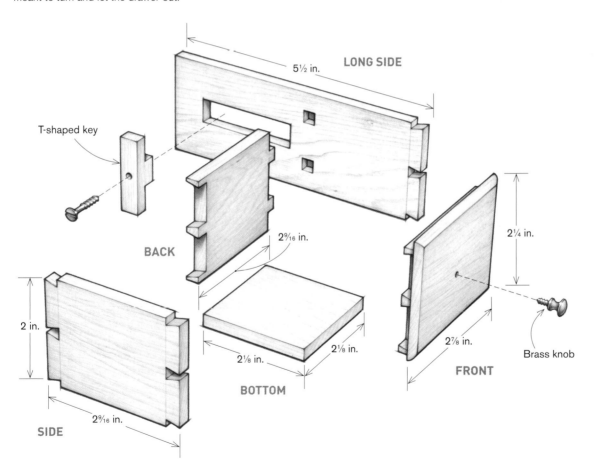

LONG SIDE — $5\frac{1}{2}$ in.

T-shaped key

BACK — $2\frac{9}{16}$ in.

SIDE — 2 in. — $2\frac{9}{16}$ in.

BOTTOM — $2\frac{1}{8}$ in. — $2\frac{1}{8}$ in.

FRONT — $2\frac{1}{4}$ in. — $2\frac{7}{8}$ in.

Brass knob

4. Crosscut the other sides to the specified lengths (see the chart on p. 91). I start with a long piece because it's much easier to cut very small pieces from large ones than from small ones. **A**

CUT THE INK-POT SIDES to finished length from a long single board. Working with small pieces on the tablesaw is not safe or easy.

LABEL EVERY JOINT on the box sides and front to keep track of what goes where (and how) as you work.

5. Rip a long piece of $^3/_8$-in.-thick stock for the front, about $^1/_4$ in. wider than the material for the sides.

6. Align the box parts and label them carefully. Only one corner gets plain old dovetails. The back of the drawer uses a mortise-and-tenon joint to connect with the long side. The front joints are stepped half-blind dovetails. **B**

Stepped Half-Blind Dovetails

The drawer front is wider and longer than the rest of the box. So you first need to cut a rabbet on the edges of the drawer front. Then you can start the half-blind dovetails.

1. Set your marking gauge to scribe at $^5/_{32}$ in., half the difference between the widths of the drawer front ($2^7/_8$ in.) and the drawer back ($2^9/_{16}$ in.). Scribe lines along the inside face of the drawer front that show where the outside edges of the sides intersect the drawer front. Do this on the sides and top edge, but not the bottom edge. These are your lines of cut to create the width of the rabbet. **A**

ON THE DRAWER FRONT (bottom piece), scribe lines that indicate the width of the drawer (top piece). These lines aren't baselines (scribe those, too), though I sometimes confuse them.

SAW THE RABBETS on the back of the drawer front on a bench hook.

2. Now set the marking gauge to the thickness of the sides. Scribe lines on the side and top edges of the drawer front from the inside face. These indicate the depth of the rabbet you'll cut.

3. Saw the rabbets on the three marked sides of the drawer front. Use a fine-tooth saw and the bench hook to make the cuts on the faces. Then clamp the workpiece in a bench vise and finish the rabbets with cuts along the edges. Please don't amble over to the tablesaw or router table for this because the workpiece is too small to cut safely. **B & C**

SAW THE EDGES of the rabbets with the drawer front in a bench vise.

4. Check the rabbets with a square and fix with a chisel or shoulder plane as necessary. You want the rabbets to be as straight and clean as possible or cutting dovetails on them will be that much harder. **D**

5. Scribe a baseline for the pins on the inside face of the drawer front only. You have to add the width of the rabbet to the thickness of the side to set the gauge properly.

6. Lay out and cut tails on the two side pieces. Use them to lay out the pins on the inside shoulder of the drawer front. **E**

CHECK THE ACCURACY of the rabbet with a square. Pare with a chisel to make corrections.

CHOP OUT THE TAILS on the fronts of the two side pieces of the drawer with a small chisel.

F

SAW THE SIDES OF THE PINS, keeping the saw angled so that the edges of the drawer front aren't marred.

7. Saw the edges of the pins at a strong angle without touching the shoulder of the drawer front. **F**

8. To remove the waste in half-blind dovetails, you have to chop the chips from the face and the edge. To get the waste in the corners you have to angle the chisel and pare carefully. If you cut these perfectly the first time, you're a woodworking superhero. If you can't fix your mistakes, then consider the first try well-spent practice and make another. When you're done, the joint should look something like that shown in the photos. **G, H, I & J**

G

CHOP CLOSE TO THE BASELINE with a chisel to begin removing the waste between the pins. Don't try to break out chips from this angle.

H

REMOVE THE CHIPS from the end with cuts parallel to the face. Use the bench hook to keep the workpiece steady.

I

TO REMOVE THE WASTE in the corners of the pins, angle the chisel and pare from the sides.

J

TEST FIT THE JOINT after you've removed the waste. You should be able to push the joint together with hand pressure alone.

Mortised Back

The long side can't be dovetailed to the back. It uses a simple mortise-and-tenon joint instead.

1. Saw two tenons on the end of the back and chop away the waste between them. **A**

2. Transfer the location of the tenons to the long side piece. **B**

A

SAW THE TENON SIDES as you would a dovetail pin, but at 90 degrees to the face of the board.

B

LAYOUT THE MORTISE HOLES using the tenons you've just cut.

3. Drill out the waste and chop the sides of the mortise straight and evenly. Chop to the center of the board from both sides to get the best results. Pare and fit the tenons into the mortises. **C**

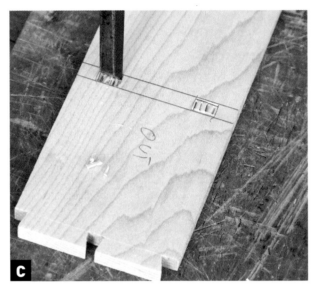

C

CHOP OUT THE MORTISES slowly, taking small chips at a time. Chop too vigorously and it's possible to split the board.

The Bottom and a Drawer Glide

A captured bottom would be best, but by now I'm sure you just want to get the job done. And there's the matter of the slot and key for the long side.

1. Assemble the four sides of the drawer. First sand the interior faces, then glue and clamp the box together. Let the glue dry.

SAW AWAY THE WASTE on the back of the T-shaped key on the tablesaw. I used a regular blade, but you could use a dado blade.

PARE THE SIDES of the key slot flat with a chisel. Remove the bulk of the waste with a drill bit.

2. Make a T-shaped key from a long blank. With a dado blade, or many passes with a regular blade, cut the arms of the key. When finished, cut the key to length, about 1½ in., on the tablesaw. **A**

3. Drill and countersink a pilot hole for a screw through the center of the key.

4. Lay out the slot according to the measurements in the drawing on p. 103, ½ in. wide and 2½ in. long. Drill away most of the waste and chop the corners with a chisel. Be very careful as you drill and make small cuts with the chisel, as it is easy to split the side. **B**

5. Measure the length and width between the sides and create a slightly oversize bottom blank.

SLIGHTLY BEVEL THE SIDES of the drawer bottom with a block plane to ensure a snug fit.

6. Trim the edges of the bottom with a handplane at a tiny angle, checking the fit into the box as you go. **C**

7. Apply a little glue to the edges and press the bottom in place.

8. After sanding and finishing, add a little brass pull to the drawer. A turned maple pull would be more authentic. However, I've not been able to find a commercial supplier of ones so small. If you have a lathe, turning one isn't too hard.

Set the Top Hinges

The edges of the box are too thin for tiny butt hinges, so use small strap hinges that screw into the box sides. You can't use the ones with stays because they only open about 100 degrees. With the angled sides of the box, they'd prevent the top from ever opening fully. Add a chain stay if you want the top to stand open.

1. Hold a hinge in place on the top edge of the box and mark the screw holes with a pencil.

2. Drill the holes with either a drill bit (if you have one small enough) or a nail with the head cut off. Be careful not to drill a hole larger than necessary.

A

SCRIBE THE OUTLINE of the strap hinges on the top edges of the box sides with a knife.

B

PARE THE SIDES of the hinge mortise to your layout line with a chisel. Test the fit of the hinge as you go.

C

WITH THE TOP RESTING on the box, transfer the location of the hinges to the top with a knife.

work SMART

Hinge screws can get loose in their holes, either from overdrilling or from moving the hinge for a better fit. The simple solution is to dab a bit of 5-minute epoxy into the hole before setting the screw. Yes, you can get the screw back out if necessary, as epoxy bonds well to the wood, but not so well to the brass.

3. Screw the hinge in place if you have extra screws. If not, hold the hinge in place. Then outline the profile of the hinge with a sharp knife or pencil. **A**

4. With a laminate trimmer and small straight bit, rout out the waste. Then trim the edges of the mortise to your layout lines with a chisel. At the curved end, use a small, tight radius gouge such as a #11. If you prefer not to use a laminate trimmer, you can chop out the waste with a small chisel. **B**

5. Repeat the process on the other side of the box. When you have both mortises done, rest the top on the box and transfer the locations of the mortises. **C**

6. Cut the mortises in the top following the same process. Be very careful not to drill through the top when you make the pilot holes for the screws, and certainly use screws shorter than 3/8 in.

Finishing Issues

Most antique Shaker furniture you see today has a very sober dark patina. However, recent research suggests that the Shakers finished and painted much of their work with bright colors, usually yellows and reds. There's a restored room at the Shaker Hancock Village in Pittsfield, Massachusetts, decorated in the happiest, brightest yellow I've ever seen, both the walls and many of the objects.

I don't suggest you paint the lap desk bright yellow. But perhaps the brightness of unstained white maple with a clear finish is more appropriately Shaker than at first glance. Be joyful with your work and let it shine.

 # Stacking Book Box

Many years ago, I found a neat project in Roy Underhill's book, *The Woodwright's Apprentice* (The University of North Carolina Press, 1996). A simple, dovetailed box with a corner miter detail that Thomas Jefferson used to store and ship his books, it immediately spoke to my heart. I had books. I was a woodworker. I made many boxes, most for books, but a few to store and transport tools. Three of them made the made the trip to India and back, keeping many of my books and hand tools safe and sound. But that's another story.

Made in poplar or pine, these book boxes are very utilitarian. But make one with cherry and you have a showpiece. Make three of them and put them on a stand and you have a lovely bookcase (see pp. 122-123). But I get ahead of myself. That's in a sidebar near the end of the chapter.

One box can make a very nice tabletop or bench-top bookcase. There's a built-in sideboard in my home's dining room where I have one packed with reference books for my kids' homework. And they're perfect for the college-bound kid.

Building them is really simple, though the joinery is a bit time consuming. The dovetails are big, many, and in ¾-in.-thick material. If you cut them by hand, you'll come away with lots of experience and a Popeye arm. The mitered ends might seem a deal breaker, as they look complex from a distance. But there's not much to them except sawing at a 45-degree angle. The hardest part is remembering that they're there and not another half pin.

Size your box around the size of your books. Some art books can be 14 in. or taller. In that case, I wouldn't make your box fully 3 ft. long unless you never plan on carrying it by yourself.

STACKING BOOK BOX

The mitered dovetails and inset handles are quiet details on this otherwise simple box. The cherry wood makes it formal, whereas in pine or poplar it would be far more utilitarian.

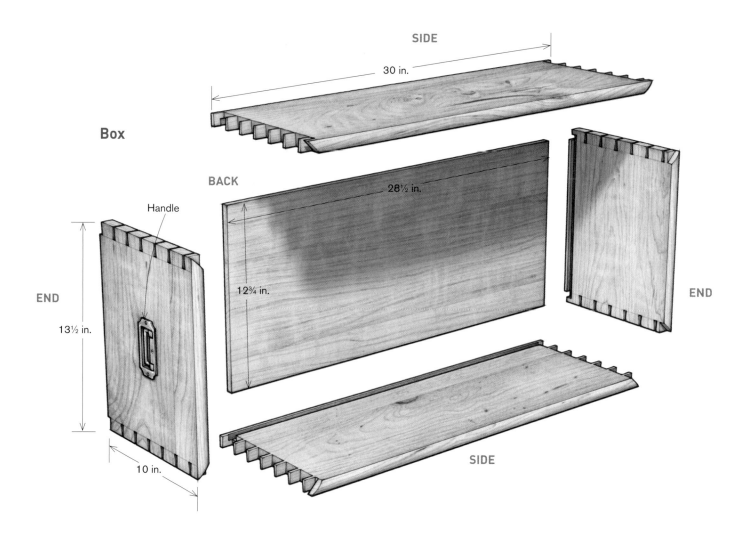

Box

SIDE
30 in.

BACK
28½ in.
12¾ in.

END
13½ in.
10 in.

Handle

END

SIDE

MATERIALS

Quantity	Part	Actual Size	Construction Notes
2	Ends	$^{13}/_{16}$ in. by 10 in. by 13½ in.	Cherry
2	Sides	$^{13}/_{16}$ in. by 10 in. by 30 in.	Cherry
1	Back	½ in. by 12¾ in. by 28½ in.	Cherry
2	Handles	½ in. by 1¾ in. by 3⅝ in.	Available from Whitechapel, Ltd. Stock number 73PMC1A 800-468-5534

SPACE BISCUIT JOINTS EVENLY but not too close to the ends of the boards. If they're too close, they may interfere with the joinery.

Stock Milling

If you have a 12-in. jointer, then by all means buy wide cherry and mill it 10 in. wide. Even if you don't have a wide jointer, it's still best to buy 10-in.-wide stock. You can rip the single boards, mill them separately, and glue them back together when they're done. This way it is fairly difficult to find the joint. If you don't have the wide stock (I didn't), gluing up different widths works just fine. Remember that the ends show and not the longer sides. So put your better boards there.

1. Crosscut enough stock for the sides and ends to rough length.

2. Pair boards according to color to get the full 10-in. width. Label the pairs on the ends where you won't lose the marks during milling. Joint and plane the lot to ³/₄-in. finished thickness.

3. Mark and cut biscuit joints on the pairs, keeping in mind the final length of the parts. You don't want to place a biscuit too close to the end where it could show. However, the further from the end you go, the less well the biscuits align the boards. Biscuit joints here are useful to align the boards in clamping. They should add little or no strength to a good glue joint between the boards. If you don't

GLUE AND CLAMP EACH SET of boards for the ends and sides. Align the clamps with the biscuit joints.

work SMART

Biscuits are not necessary for strength across an edge joint. In this application, they simply make alignment during glue-up much easier.

have a biscuit jointer, just glue the boards together, minding that they align well as you clamp. **A**

4. Edge glue each pair of boards, applying glue and biscuits. Set the clamps across the biscuits, not between, as the direct clamping pressure tends to make a better joint. Let the boards dry for 24 hours. **B**

5. Rough-sand the glued-up sides and ends, cleaning off the machine marks and glue squeeze-out. Depending on how much tearout is on the surface, I'll start with 100-grit or even 80-grit sandpaper, as cherry is a hard wood. Sand up to 120-grit, but not finer. You'll handle the boards quite a bit before assembly. Just before then is the best time to finish-sand.

work SMART

For edge joints, always let the glue dry at least a day before working the surface. This is because the glue's moisture can swell the wood around the joint. If you sand or plane the surface when it's swollen, you may end up with a little groove along the joint.

LABEL THE JOINTS after you set up the box with the sides and ends oriented as you wish. Also indicate which sides face out.

6. Rip all four boards 10 in. wide. Crosscut them to final length. Exact length isn't as important as having both sides and both ends match.

Mitered Dovetails at Corners

You may laugh, but this is a very simple joint to cut. Sure, it's easier the tenth time you try it rather than the first; but even on the first go there's not much of a challenge. It just looks difficult. I admit that I cut the pins very small here because they look lovely, and that's harder to do than wide pins. So make the pins wider, as in Chapter 3 (see p. 36), and you're set. The mitered corners frankly don't add much complexity, except that you just have to remember to cut a miter at the ends and not another half pin.

1. Set the sides and ends on edge and mark each corner joint with letters, numbers, or some system to tell them apart. Also write "outside" on the faces. **A**

SCRIBE A BASELINE for the dovetails on the faces and bottom edge of all the boards, but not on the top edge (where you'll put the miter).

2. Scribe a baseline across each board for the dovetails. Scribe on the bottom edge, but not on the top, where you'll cut the miter. **B**

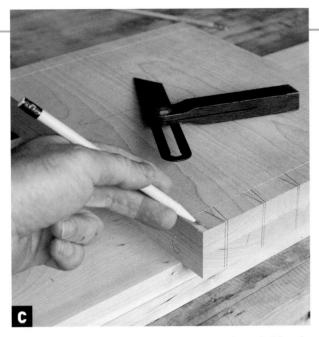

C

WHEN YOU LAY OUT THE TAILS, leave approximately 1 in. of space between the top edge and the last pin for the miter joint. It should look like a large half-tail.

E

SAW YOUR MITER LINE without sawing into the face of the board. It doesn't matter if you saw on or to one side of the line.

D

DRAW THE MITER ANGLES on the top edges. Also scribe a straight line across the ends about ⅜ in. to ½ in. from the top. This line describes the bottom of the miter.

3. Lay out as many tails as you like, anywhere from three to as many as you can fit. At the top edge, instead of laying out a half pin, leave about an inch of space for the miters. I cut six full tails, a nice compromise between looks and work. **C**

4. Lay out the mitered corners by first drawing a straight line on the ends of the boards about ⅜ in. from the top edge. On the inside face, drop the line straight to the baseline. Then draw a 45-degree angle on the top edge. This should go exactly from the baseline to the corner. Be careful to draw the line the right way, from the interior baseline to the exterior corner. **D**

5. Cut your tails with a fine-toothed saw. For the miter, first cut on the straight lines at a 45-degree angle, careful to not cut into the outside face of the board. **E** Then cut along the 45-degree line on the top edge of the board, staying just a bit inside the line. **F** (on p. 116)

F

FROM ABOVE, SAW on the waste side of your miter line and remove the triangular piece of waste.

G

DRILL OUT THE WASTE between tails, either with a cordless drill or on a drill press. It's faster than chopping.

6. Chop out the waste between the tails, as shown in Chapter 3 (see p. 38), using a small chisel. However, you can also save time and effort by first drilling out the waste. If you try this, be very careful not to let the drill wander and cut below the baseline or into the side of the tails. Drill halfway through from each side. **G**

7. If you cut the tails for small pins, you may not be able to fit the pencil down into the space between the tails to mark the tops of the pins. In this case, first mark the top of the pin from the outside with the tail board on top. Also mark the location of the miter (a pencil fits under easily). **H**

8. Clamp the tail and pin boards together (inside face to inside face) so that the baseline of the tail board aligns with the top edge of the pin board. Mark where the bottom corners of the tails intersect the tail board. To lay out the tops of the pins, simply connect the points at the front and back. Also drop a straight line for the miter from the layout line on the end of the board. **I & J**

H

TRANSFER THE FRONT of the pin locations to the face of the pin board. You can't reach inside with a pencil.

TRANSFER THE BACK of the pin locations to the end of the pin board. Clamp the tail board against the pin board in a bench vise to align them while you do this.

CONNECT YOUR LAYOUT MARKS for the front and back of the pins with a straightedge and pencil.

9. Saw out the pins as in Chapter 3 (see p. 39), just inside your layout lines to ensure a tight fit. For the mitered corner, also saw inside your lines straight down (there's no need to tilt the saw for this cut). Then turn the board sideways in the vise and cut the 45-degree end. **K**

10. Chop out the waste between the pins. I sometimes use a bandsaw to cut out the waste. It's faster but also easier to make mistakes. Pare the waste right to the baseline with a sharp chisel. Then

test-fit the joint, paring the faces of the pins where necessary to get a good fit. Treat the sides of the miters in the same fashion, paring them until they fit just right as the joint comes together. Only when the joint is together can you see if the faces of the miters need adjustment to fit well. Pare the high points until they fit tight when the tails touch the baseline of the pin board. **L**

SAW OUT THE OPPOSING miter waste the same way as on the tail board.

WHEN TESTING THE FIT, check alignment of the sides of the miters as well.

CUT A GROOVE ALONG the bottom of the box with a router and rabbeting bit. Dry-assemble the box first to make routing the corners much easier.

CHOP OUT THE CORNERS of the groove to accept a rectangular bottom panel.

A Groove for the Bottom and Edge Molding

A captured ¾-in.-plywood bottom works best for these boxes if you plan on using them to transport heavy objects. You can size it to fit exactly and glue it in the groove for added strength. But if you're only making one box, it's a waste (and expensive) to buy an entire sheet of plywood. A solid wood bottom can work fine, though you shouldn't make it as wide or glue it in the groove.

1. Dry-assemble the box and turn it upside down. If necessary, plane or sand the corners flush. If the corners aren't flush, the router base will get hung up when you cut the groove in the next step.

2. With a ½-in.-wide rabbeting bit that cuts ⅜ in. deep, cut a groove in the box insides, ¼ in. from the bottom edge. Make sure the box is stable and either clamped to the bench or resting on a nonslip surface. When cutting along the edge, away from the corners, the router can tilt to one side making an uneven groove. Position your body so that you don't have to lean as you cut. Make many shallow cuts rather than one deep cut for best results. **A**

3. Disassemble the box and chop out the rounded corners in the grooves. You can also round the corners of the bottom panel. But sometimes gaps can show, so it's best to chop out the corners. **B**

4. Measure the inside dimensions from the inside of the grooves and make a bottom panel from ¾-in. plywood. So the panel will fit in the ½-in. groove, cut a ¼-in. rabbet on the edges on a router table or on the tablesaw.

CUT A MILD BULLNOSE EDGE on the top of the box sides with a large quarter-round bit in a router table. Make cuts from both sides.

5. With a large quarter-round bit, mold the top edge of the bookcase. I like a flattened bullnose that's cut from both sides on the router table. But choose the profile you like, making test boards to ensure good results. A beaded edge would also be attractive. **C**

6. To smooth the bullnose, stretch sandpaper over the edge and sand. I use worn-out sanding disks for this work. **D**

Assembly

If you use plywood for the bottom panel, you can glue it in the groove for greater structural integrity.

1. Before assembly, finish-sand the inside faces of the box and the molded edge to 180-grit or 220-grit. Be careful not to sand or round over the pins or tails. You can make well-fitting joinery loose by over-aggressive sanding.

2. Apply glue on the pins and in the groove of each piece.

SAND THE BULLNOSE by wrapping a piece of sandpaper over the edge. Do not sand past the ends, as you can spoil the miter joints.

3. There's an order of assembly that's important. First, capture the bottom panel between the two long sides. Then slide in place one of the ends, finally the other. Yellow and white glue get tacky very quickly, so you might need a mallet to set the joinery tight before clamping. Polyurethane glues aren't tacky at first and make assembly a bit easier, but either glue is fine.

ASSEMBLE THE BOX with yellow glue in the joints. If the joints don't fit perfectly flush with a few taps of a deadblow hammer, use clamps.

4. If the pins don't stick out past the tails, you can add clamps to hold things tight while the glue dries. If the pins are long, you can still use clamps, just offset them from the joints a little and use light pressure. Otherwise you'll bow the sides. **A**

5. When the glue dries, finish-sand the exterior up through 220-grit. If the corner moldings don't line up perfectly, use a sharp chisel and sandpaper to even the joint. **B**

Fitting Inset Handles

The handles are optional. They're a good-looking addition and useful, but books still fit in the boxes without them. You can set them flush with the surface of the box, or set them partially so the profile stands 1/16 in. proud. This is the easier way to do it and I think it looks just as good. If you plan on moving the boxes around often, use a beefier handle style. The one I used is a little more pretty than strong.

1. Figure out the size and shape of the mortise you need to seat the handle. Measure the back of the handle, considering the screws that hold the backing plate in place. **A**

PARE FLUSH SLIGHTLY MISALIGNED joints with a sharp chisel and sandpaper.

MEASURE THE BODY of the handle in length, width, and depth.

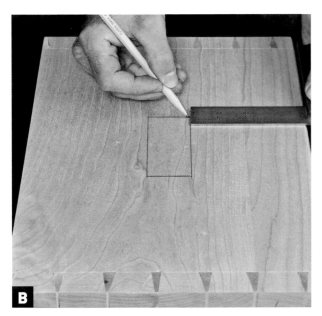

LAY OUT THE MORTISE for the body of the handle centered on the end of the box.

2. Lay out the mortise, centered on the box end. **B**

3. Remove the waste with a ¼-in. straight bit in a router. **C**

4. These particular handles have screws on the back that are proud and require some additional shaping of the mortise. Cut these details with a chisel, testing the fit of the handle as you go. **D**

5. Set the handles with steel screws (save the brass screws for a final fitting). Then remove the handles for finishing.

Finishing

For these book boxes, I would not use a film finish if I planned on moving them around. Chips will be the inevitable consequence. On the other hand, an oil and wax finish is not ideal either. If you wax the interior, it will get on the books. If your collection is disposable paperbacks, then this isn't a concern. And you can always wax only the exterior. But all in all, my preferred finish is a thin wipe-on varnish. It won't chip and there's no need for wax.

CUT THE MORTISE FOR THE HANDLE with a router and plunge bit. Cut right to your layout line and don't worry about small errors, as it will all be hidden.

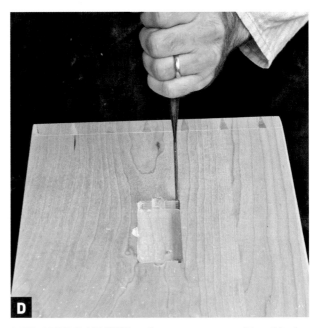

CHOP OUT THE CORNERS and screw recesses with a chisel. Make adjustments as necessary until the handle flanges sit flush against the box side.

TWO BASES FOR THREE BOXES

Although these boxes are wonderfully useful on their own, they do benefit from a dedicated stand. There are many good configurations depending on how many you want to stack, but to keep things simple, here are two ideas for a stack of three boxes.

The first is a side table tailor fit to the boxes. The second is a simple, low kick stand made from cherry plywood or solid wood.

I've found that once the boxes are loaded with books, they don't move. However, if you

BOOK STAND

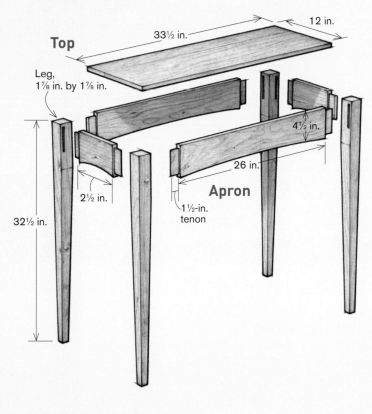

Top

33½ in.

12 in.

Leg, 1⅞ in. by 1⅞ in.

4½ in.

2½ in.

26 in.

Apron

1½-in. tenon

32½ in.

ELEGANT AND POISED on a graceful table, the book boxes will have a presence in almost any room.

have small children or simply worry that they're not secured, you can connect them in any number of ways. The more secure the connection, however, the less portable the boxes become.

The easiest connection method is to attach flat brass straps across the box backs and table. I use this method if the boxes are up against a wall. Otherwise, hidden screws (countersunk and plugged) inside the boxes are a strong, if permanent, solution.

A SIMPLE KICK STAND gives the book boxes a utilitarian presence, perfect next to a desk.

KICK STAND

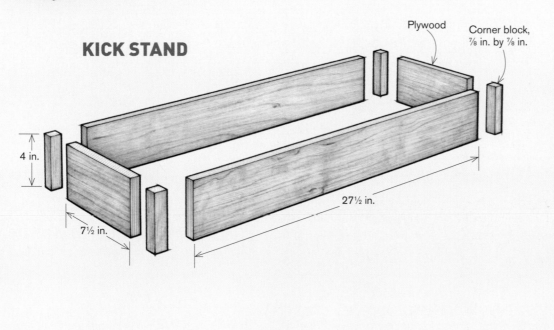

Plywood

Corner block, ⅞ in. by ⅞ in.

4 in.

7½ in.

27½ in.

8 Jewelry Box

t's staggering to think that complex jewelry boxes have been around for millennia. Years ago, I saw an Egyptian cosmetics box in a museum. Though it was 5,000 years old, the sides and top were frames-and-panels. It had several drawers, beautifully dovetailed. The top lid had metal hinges. Inside were divided compartments, nesting trays, and other refined details.

There really isn't anything new under the sun, nor in this jewelry box, which is very simple compared to that Egyptian one. However, a certain level of complexity is part of jewelry box territory. You need a place for necklaces, a different one for rings, another for earrings, a place for bracelets, a place for, well, you name it. And not all necklaces are the same length, or rings the same size. No one compartment or holder can store them all.

More than any other box, you want to design a jewelry box's compartments to hold specific pieces. Measure the length of the necklaces. Measure the size of the rings. Count them all. Then build the box around them rather than following the specifications here. If the drawers don't close because your rings are too big, I don't want to hear about it.

But even more important than the practical storage of jewelry, a good jewelry box should be as special as the person it's for. As a rule, I start with a fancier-than-usual wood. The wood for this box came from a very special old maple; much of the wood shows compression curl and other interesting grain (see "Furniture From Your Backyard Trees" on p. 142 on milling your own lumber). The box design doesn't come from any particular tradition. You could say the slightly tapered posts are Egyptian in influence, but perhaps they're upside-down Shaker table legs. Most of all, the jewelry box was designed for convenience, with necklaces hanging in side compartments and many small drawers so that the clutter never gets too deep.

JEWELRY BOX

This jewelry box has three drawers, two necklace compartments behind doors on the sides, and another compartment under the center part of the top. The drawers are lined with felt. Hooks in the side compartments hold the necklaces in place. It's made of maple from a very old tree.

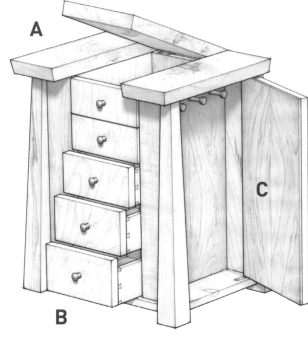

A

B

C

A Box Carcass

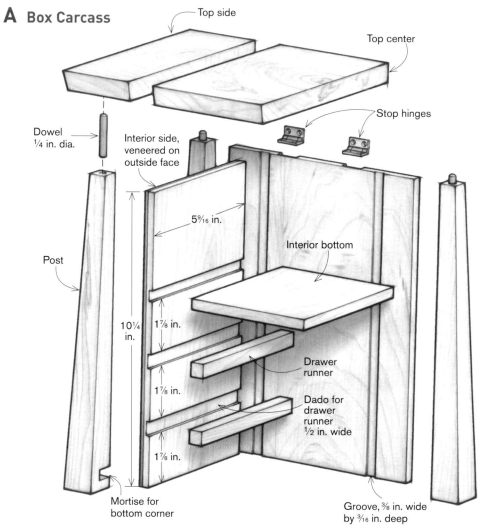

Top side

Top center

Stop hinges

Dowel
¼ in. dia.

Interior side,
veneered on
outside face

5⁹⁄₁₆ in.

Interior bottom

Post

10¼
in.

1⅞ in.

1⅞ in.

Drawer
runner

Dado for
drawer
runner
½ in. wide

1⅞ in.

Mortise for
bottom corner

Groove, ⅜ in. wide
by ³⁄₁₆ in. deep

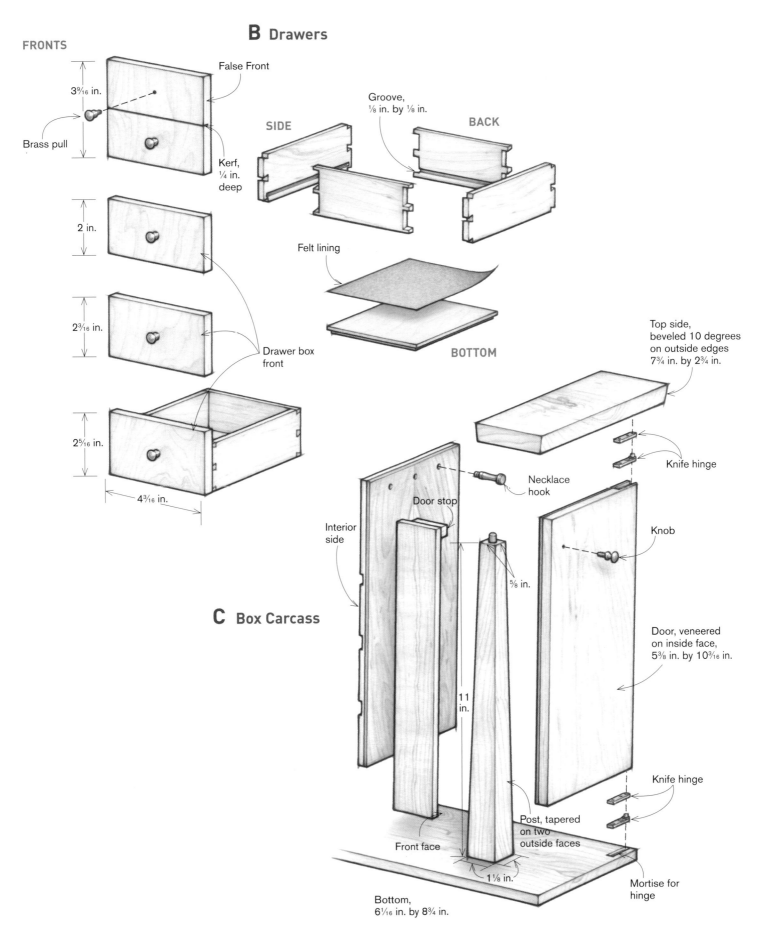

FRONTS

B Drawers

$3^9/_{16}$ in.

False Front

Brass pull

Kerf, $1/_4$ in. deep

2 in.

$2^3/_{16}$ in.

$2^5/_{16}$ in.

Drawer box front

$4^3/_{16}$ in.

SIDE

Groove, $1/_8$ in. by $1/_8$ in.

BACK

Felt lining

BOTTOM

Top side, beveled 10 degrees on outside edges $7^3/_4$ in. by $2^3/_4$ in.

Knife hinge

Interior side

Necklace hook

Door stop

Knob

C Box Carcass

$5/_8$ in.

Door, veneered on inside face, $5^3/_8$ in. by $10^3/_{16}$ in.

11 in.

Knife hinge

Front face

Post, tapered on two outside faces

Mortise for hinge

$1^1/_8$ in.

Bottom, $6^1/_{16}$ in. by $8^3/_4$ in.

MATERIALS

Quantity	Part	Actual Size	Construction Notes
1	Back	$3/8$ in. by $7^7/16$ in. by $10^5/8$ in.	Maple
2	Interior sides	$3/8$ in. by $5^9/16$ in. by $10^1/4$ in.	Maple
1	Bottom	$3/8$ in. by $6^1/16$ in. by $8^3/4$ in.	Maple
2	Front faces	$5/16$ in. by $1^5/8$ in. by $10^1/4$ in.	Maple
1	Top	$11/16$ in. by $7^3/4$ in. by $9^3/4$ in.	Maple; start with rough size board, 10 in. long, cut into three parts
4	Posts	$1^1/8$ in. by $1^1/8$ in. by 11 in.	Maple
2	Doors	$5/16$ in. by $5^3/8$ in. by $10^3/16$ in.	Maple
1	Interior bottom	$3/8$ in. by $4^1/2$ in. by $5^7/16$ in.	Maple
4	Runners	$1/2$ in. by $1/2$ in. by $5^1/2$ in.	Maple
1	False drawer front	$7/16$ in. by $4^3/16$ in. by $3^9/16$ in.	Maple; start with rough size board, 12 in. long
1	Top drawer front	$7/16$ in. by $4^3/16$ in. by 2 in.	Maple
1	Middle drawer front	$7/16$ in. by $4^3/16$ in. by $2^3/16$ in.	Maple
1	Bottom drawer front	$7/16$ in. by $4^3/16$ in. by $2^5/16$ in.	Maple
6	Drawer box sides	$1/4$ in. by $1^3/4$ in. by $5^5/16$ in.	Maple
6	Drawer box fronts and backs	$1/4$ in. by $1^3/4$ in. by $4^1/8$ in.	Maple
6	Drawer bottoms	$1/4$ in. by $3^7/8$ in. by 5 in.	Maple
2	Door stops	$3/8$ in. by $3/8$ in. by $1^3/16$ in.	Maple
1	Drawer front blank	$7/16$ in. by $4^3/16$ in. by 11 in.	Maple; rough length for all five drawer fronts.
	Veneer for doors and interior sides	2 sq. ft. by $1/8$ in. thick	Apple wood or other
7	Knobs		Available from Whitechapel, Ltd.; Stock number 247HV12; 800-468-5534
6	Necklace hooks		Available from Brusso, Inc.; Stock number MC 437; 212-337-8510
2	Top hinges		Available from Brusso, Inc.; Stock number JB-101 or JB-102
1	Felt lining	1 ft. by 2 ft.	Available from Rockler, Inc.; Stock number 22822; 800-279-4441
1	Padded ring holder		Available from Rockler, Inc.; Stock number 35248
4	Felt foot pads		Available at local home centers and hardware stores.
4	Dowels	$1/4$ in. dia. by $1^1/8$ in.	

Milling Maple Stock

Maple moves when you work it. Mill it on Monday and it twists on Tuesday. The best solution is a time-consuming milling schedule, so I don't recommend being in a hurry. I'll admit another solution is to use a different wood.

1. Make a list of all the parts you'll need for the box. Go through the lumber you have for the project and choose boards for specific tasks. Take the nicest grain for the top, sides, and drawer fronts, and leave the lackluster pieces for drawer bottoms and other less-seen pieces. Of course you have to make concessions for size and shape.

GLUED-UP LEGS WITHOUT SEAMS

A

CLAMP 2-IN.-WIDE BOARDS together face to face to create thicker stock.

B

JOINT NEW FACES on the edges of the boards at 45 degrees.

For such a small project, it doesn't make sense to buy a whole board of 5/4 maple. It takes some work, but there's a good way to make the posts for this project from 4/4 stock. It effectively hides the seam between the boards so they look like solid wood.

1. Joint and plane two pieces of 4/4 stock to ⅞ -in. or ¹³⁄₁₆-in. thickness, about 2 in. wide and at least 12 in. long for each post.

2. Glue and clamp the pairs face to face. Let the glue dry until rubbery. **A**

3. Tilt your jointer's fence to 45 degrees and cut a bevel that reaches the seam between the boards. If your jointed face isn't parallel to the line of the seam, make partial cuts on the jointer to align it.

4. Cut a matching bevel on the opposite side that also reaches the seam. **B**

C

RIP THE BLANKS SQUARE and to width on the tablesaw.

5. Rip the remaining sides to 1⅛-in. width. **C**

The seams between the boards are effectively hidden at the edges. When you taper these posts, just make sure you cut so the seam still follows the edge.

I chose a piece with a knot and feather grain for the top.

2. Crosscut pieces to length and rip them to oversize width. Add 1/4 in. to small pieces and 1/2 in. to wider ones. Mill two or three extra pieces just in case. Milling everything all at once is important for efficiency and sanity. In the middle of a project, it's frustrating to have to mill extra pieces and wait a few days for them to warp.

3. Joint and plane everything to oversize thickness, about 1/8 in. extra. Stack the boards on edge for two or three days with air on both sides. This will allow them to warp before you mill them to final thickness. Still, with maple you may find pieces warp after you finish them. Thankfully, in a small box minor twists aren't too important.

4. As you need the various parts indicated in the steps that follow, cut them to finished length and

sand them as necessary. By and large, you'll want to finish-sand all the parts to 220-grit, though leave the edges jointed straight and smooth. Sanding is especially important for the drawer glides and inside faces of the interior sides.

Tapering the Posts

All four posts are identical, having two tapered faces. Make them from a single piece of 5/4 maple. If you don't have wood that size or don't want to buy a whole board, you can make posts from thinner stock (see "Glued-Up Legs Without Seams" on p. 129).

1. Lay out the tapers on the post stock, 1 1/8 in. square and 11 in. long. The taper lines should run the length of the post from the bottom outside corner of the post to a mark 5/8 in. from the inside edge at the opposite end. Do this on two sides.

A

CUT THE TAPERS on a bandsaw, keeping outside your layout line. It's easier to start the cut at the top than at the bottom.

SAND THE BANDSAWN FACES of each post smooth and flat on a stationary belt sander. This tool helps keep the sanded surfaces straight, flat, and square.

I find it helpful to draw a ⅝-in. square on the top of the post to keep track of the faces on which the layout lines should go.

2. Saw the tapers on a bandsaw. I leave the layout line rather than splitting it. It helps to keep the line for the next step. **A**

3. Sand the tapered faces of the post on a stationary belt sander. This tool will keep thin and flat surfaces flat. Hand sanders will round the faces. You can also use a portable belt sander if you secure the workpiece to a bench top. And sandpaper wrapped around a block works very well, but takes longer. **B**

Veneering the Necklace Compartment

I veneered the necklace compartment on the inside with some small pieces of apple wood. I made the veneer from a tree in my backyard. But don't fret if this isn't an option (making and preparing your own veneer takes special tools and a long time). Commercial veneer of any species will work just fine. The real trouble is clamping the veneer while the glue sets. You need either a press or a whole lot of very strong clamps. You can always skip this step if you prefer. Just mill the door ⅛ in. thicker.

1. Make or buy enough ⅛-in.-thick veneer to cover one door blank at least four times. I use thicker veneer for two reasons. One is that exposed edges tend not to chip away (the veneer edge on the doors is exposed). Second, I think there's less chance of warping from one-sided veneering. The rule with thin veneers is to always do to one side what you do to the other. But as the ⅛-in.-thick veneer is almost half the thickness of the door, the two sides should keep each other in check.

HOMEGROWN VENEER

The apple wood veneer for this box was homemade. If that makes you shrug, just buy commercial veneer. But here's how to do it if you're interested. The only specialty equipment you need is a bandsaw.

Cut a limb from a promising tree, such as an apple tree. Cut a manageable length from the limb, no more than two or three feet. Joint a flat surface about 1 in. to 2 in. wide on one side of the limb. Now joint a second face at 90 degrees to the first. It's fine if the two flat faces don't connect perfectly at an edge.

At the bandsaw, set the blade ⅛ in. (or a little more) from the fence and take a slice off your limb. There's your first piece of veneer. Joint the sawn face on the limb again to make it smooth. Repeat this process until you've cut up the whole limb.

To dry the veneer pieces, wrap them tightly in string and toss the bundle in the corner of the shop for a few months. They'll warp a bit, and probably split at the ends, but I still get a lot of useable veneer from this method.

JOINT THE INSIDE EDGES of your veneer straight and square.

DRAW THE OUTLINE of the doors and interior sides on the veneer to size it correctly.

2. If the veneer pieces are too small to cover an entire door or side, you'll need to use two pieces. Joint the inside edges of the pieces straight and true. **A**

3. Set your veneer pieces together in pairs (I book-matched mine because I think it looks good). Align the doors and interior sides over the veneer pieces and scribe their outline. **B**

4. Cut away the veneer waste on either the tablesaw or bandsaw so the veneer is the same size as the door and interior sides.

5. If you're using two pieces of veneer for each panel, tape the veneer together to get a tight joint between the pieces. I use blue painter's tape on the faces of the veneer.

6. Apply a thin layer of polyurethane or a specialized veneer glue to the backs of the veneer pieces and clamp them in place. If you have a veneer press, by all means use it. If not, find a way to apply even clamping pressure across the whole face of the veneer (while keeping the panel flat). Pieces of sanded plywood make good cauls, but remember to apply clamping pressure in the center as well, not just along the edges.

7. When the glue sets, joint, rip, and crosscut each panel to finished dimensions. Finish-sand them as well.

Assembling the Interior Sides and Back

Unlike most of the other boxes in this book, you build this one from the inside out. This is because the sides are really doors and the front has drawers.

1. Cut two grooves on the inside face of the back. The grooves should be exactly as wide as the interior sides you just finished veneering, $^3/_8$ in. thick and about $^3/_{16}$ in. deep. The grooves should be located about $1^1/_8$ in. from the sides of the back. I use a dado blade in my tablesaw for this, though a router with a straight bit also works well. **A**

2. Check the fit of the interior sides in the grooves. Widen the grooves until the sides fit snug. **B**

A

CUT GROOVES ON THE INSIDE FACE of the back for the interior sides. Use the same fence setting for both sides to keep them centered.

3. Drill three holes for the necklace hooks along the top edge of each side. Space the holes evenly, about 1 in. below the edge. This will allow space for fingers to reach in and pick necklaces off the hooks. I do this on a drill press because I want the row of hooks to stand evenly. If you drill the post holes with a hand drill, the posts may stand at slightly different angles. However, if you don't drill them evenly, no worries—they're thankfully hard to see in the finished box. **C**

4. Cut dados on the inside faces of the interior sides. Again, I use the tablesaw and a dado blade for this operation, though a router with a straight bit is also good. Two of the dados are for drawer

B

TEST THE SIDES in the grooves, widening them until you get a snug fit.

C

DRILL HOLES FOR THE NECKLACE HOOKS. Use a drill bit the exact diameter of the hook base.

CUT THE DADOS in the interior sides on the table-saw. Use the rip fence as a guide but take extra precautions to keep the workpiece tight against the miter gauge and move it straight in the cut.

CLAMP THE DRAWER RUNNERS in the two lower dados. They should be flush with the front edge and 3/16 in. shy of the back edge.

runners. The third and top one is for the bottom of the top compartment. The dados should each be about 1/2 in. wide. The top one should be sized to the thickness of the interior bottom (for the top compartment) and 3/16 in. deep. **D**

5. Make and test fit drawer runners in the dados. They should be the full width of the interior sides, be flush with the front edge, and end 3/16 in. or more from the box back. This is because one edge of the interior sides should fit into the grooves in the back. **E**

6. Sizing the interior bottom is a bit tricky. If you make it too small or too big, the whole box will become trapezoidal. I've given the dimensions for mine in the chart on p. 128, but confirm yours from real measurements. To get them, mock up the interior sides in the back grooves. Then measure between the two dados in the interior sides to get the width of the interior bottom. Make a bottom that fits well and makes the sides square to the back.

7. Glue up the back, two interior sides, and interior bottom at the same time. Apply a little glue in each of the grooves and dados (but not so much that you get squeeze-out). Clamp as you can and then check that the sides are square to the back. **F**

8. Glue and clamp the front faces to the edges of the interior sides. They should be flush with the interior of the box and project the same distance from the face of the interior sides as the back does. If they're not the same, then the necklace compartment won't be rectangular. As long as the pieces are flat and smooth, the glue joints between them will be perfectly strong on their own. **G**

9. Glue and clamp the rear posts to the edges of the back. Align the legs flush with the inside face of the back. The slight taper can make it hard to clamp the posts in place. Sometimes a little blue tape on the face of the clamp prevents sliding. The box is starting to take shape, though it's not yet box-shaped. **H**

GLUE AND CLAMP the front faces to the interior sides. Watch that clamping pressure doesn't make them slide out of position before the glue grips.

GLUE AND CLAMP TOGETHER the interior sides, interior bottom, and back. Check that they're square relative to one another and adjust before the glue sets.

GLUE AND CLAMP the rear posts to the back. Watch that your clamps don't slide on the tapered posts and lessen their pressure.

USE A STRAIGHTEDGE to draw a straight line on the bottom from the front face to the back. It should intersect exactly between back and post.

LAY OUT THE LOCATIONS of the knife hinges in the bottom to the outside of the layout line you just marked.

The Box Bottom

Much like the interior sides, there's much to do to the bottom before you attach it.

1. Center the bottom piece (milled to final dimensions) under the box and flush with the back. Mark a straight line between the edge of the front face and the joint between the rear post and the back. This line indicates where the side door will be located. **A**

2. Lay out the location for the knife hinges on the bottom. The bottom leaf should be about $1/16$ in. from the back edge and aligned with the outside of your layout line. **B**

3. Use a laminate trimmer to cut out the waste between your lines. The mortise should be just as deep as the hinge is thick. Cut close to, but not over, your layout lines. **C**

4. Pare or chop right to your layout lines with a chisel, though leave the pencil lines intact for a tight fit. A #5 gouge is useful to clean up the curved end. As you pare, test-fit the hinge until it fits. **D**

REMOVE THE WASTE for the knife hinges with a laminate trimmer. Don't cut past the layout lines.

PARE THE KNIFE-HINGE MORTISE sides straight with a sharp chisel. Leave the layout lines intact for a tight fit.

DRILL THREE PILOT HOLES on either side in the bottom inside the layout lines that show where the interior sides will intersect. Use a 3d nail with its head cut off as a bit.

5. With the bottom aligned under the box again, outline the intersection of the interior sides and front faces with a pencil.

6. Cut the head off a 3d nail and use it to drill a few pilot holes in the bottom. Space the holes a few inches apart and center them where the interior sides will intersect. **E**

7. Cut the tips off the nails you'll use to attach the bottom, making them shorter. They only need to be about ⅝ in. long. The blunt tips also reduce splitting.

8. To attach the bottom, run glue along its back edge, where it will intersect the back and posts. It's a cross-grain joint, but will still add a little strength to the box.

9. With the bottom clamped in place, nail it to the interior sides. With all the nails in place, set the nails. There's no point using glue, as it's an end-grain joint. Conceivably, you could use epoxy, but there's not much gain in overall strength, as the bottom will be held in place by the front posts. **F**

WITH THE BOTTOM GLUED and clamped to the back, set the nails that hold the bottom to the sides.

SET YOUR MARKING GAUGE to the thickness of the bottom with the fence ³⁄₈ in. from the inside pin.

SAW THE EDGES of the mortises in the front posts at a 45-degree angle.

Fit the Front Posts

A mortise in the front post captures the corner of the bottom.

1. On a two-pin marking gauge, set the distance between the pins to the thickness of the bottom, and set the fence about ³⁄₈ in. from the inside pin. If your gauge has only one pin, you just need to set and use it twice to scribe the two lines for each side of the mortise. **A**

2. With the marking gauge, scribe lines on the front posts where the bottom of the box will intersect the inside corners of the posts. Measure for the ends of the mortises and mark them with a pencil. The mortise should be ⁵⁄₈ in. long on each side.

3. Cut the faces of the mortises with a fine-toothed saw. To do this on the tablesaw would require a jig so I don't bother. **B**

4. Drill out the waste between your layout lines. Then chop and pare the rest with a chisel to make a square mortise in each post. Take small bites as the mortise is close to the end of the post. If you're too aggressive you can split off the end. **C**

CHOP OUT THE MORTISE WASTE with a small chisel, taking small cuts each time.

5. Test the fit of the mortise on the corner of the bottom as you go. You want the post to slide snugly over the corner and sit flush against the edge of the front face.

6. Apply glue to the edges of the front faces and clamp the posts in place. There's no need to glue the mortises, as their strength is mechanical. **D**

GLUE AND CLAMP the front posts to the front faces. The bottom should fit snugly into the mortises in each post.

Milling the Top

Though the finished top is in three pieces, start with an oversized single piece. The continuous grain will look good when the box is closed.

1. To end up with a top about 9¾ in. long, start with a blank about 10 in. long. You'll lose ¼ in. of length (if your tablesaw cuts an ⅛-in. kerf) when you cut the top into three parts.

2. Bevel the front and side edges at about 10 degrees. I didn't bevel the back because I think it looks better. Bevel it if you want to, though. You might like it better. **A**

3. Saw the top into three parts. The two ends should be 2¹¹⁄₁₆ in. long, and the center should end up at 4⅜ in. Remember to adjust your tablesaw blade back to 90 degrees to do this. **B**

BEVEL THE EDGES of the top by 10 degrees on the tablesaw.

CUT THE TOP into three pieces with the blade set at 90 degrees. Cut the two sides to the same length, 2¹¹⁄₁₆ in.

C

OUTLINE THE PROFILE of the box on the underside of the top pieces. Mark where the top intersects the joint between post and back.

D

LAY OUT THE KNIFE-HINGE mortises in the top side pieces.

4. Finish-sand the three pieces. Take special care to keep the inside edges straight. They'll form a visual joint when the top is closed.

5. Center the box upside down on the underside of the three top pieces. With a pencil, outline where the box intersects the top. With special care, mark the joint between the rear post and back. You need this location to align the top knife hinge properly. **C**

6. Lay out the knife hinges on the undersides of the tops. They go in the same place relative to the back and rear post that the ones on the bottom of the box do. **D**

7. Cut the mortises the same way you cut them in the bottom.

Joinery for the Top

The top can't just be glued into place because the mating surfaces are all end grain. Nailing with decorative nails is an option for a more rustic look, but I used hidden dowels.

1. Set the top sides in place and align them precisely. Put layout marks at the back and front so that you can see easily. These will help you put the top back in the same place when you set it on the dowel centers. This alignment is crucial for the hinges. **A**

MARK ON THE BACK AND TOP EXACTLY WHERE THE TOP RESTS. These marks will help you orient the top when you set the dowels.

WITH DOWEL CENTERS IN PLACE, align the top sides on the box as best you can by your layout marks.

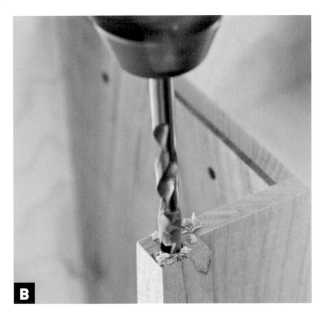

DRILL DOWEL HOLES straight down into the tops of the posts about ¾ in. deep.

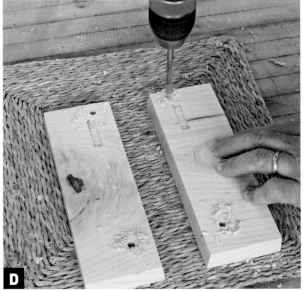

DRILL THE OPPOSITE dowel holes in the top sides about ⅜ in. to ½ in. deep.

2. Drill ¼-in.-dia. holes in the tops of the posts, about ¾ in. deep if you're using 1⅛-in.-long dowels. A drill press is best for this job, but holding a hand drill carefully will get the holes straight enough. **B**

3. Set dowel centers in the holes and then place the top over them, aligned as precisely as you can. Press down to mark the dowel locations on the underside of the top. **C**

4. Drill opposite holes in the top sides, about ⅜ in. or ½ in. deep. Use the quill depth stop on a drill press or tape on the drill bit to avoid drilling through. **D**

5. Make sure the tops fit properly on the box and align with your layout marks. You can adjust a little bit by shaving the dowel. But don't glue them in place just yet because you have to fit and finish the doors and the rest of the box first.

PARE THE HINGE-MORTISE walls straight with a chisel. You're cutting with the grain.

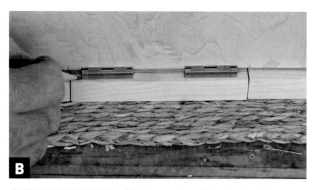

OUTLINE THE HINGES with the center of the top in place. Make sure the gaps between the top center and side pieces are even.

Mortising for Hinges

The butt hinges for the center of the top are set in end grain. For such a small top, there's no need to worry about loss of strength. I used Brusso JB-103 hinges here because I had them. Smaller hinges, such as the JB-102 or JB-101, are a more suitable size. For more details about the process of setting them, see Chapter 5 (p. 78).

1. Align the hinges in the back of the top center of the lid, and mark their locations.

2. Cut out the waste with a laminate trimmer. Pare the mortises to their layout lines and fit the hinges in place. **A**

3. Fit the two side top pieces with dowels and dry fit them.

4. Center the top between the two side pieces and mark the hinge locations. Also outline the backs of the hinges. **B**

FURNITURE FROM YOUR BACKYARD TREES

It's a common question I get: "Can I make something out of an old tree in my backyard?" The answer is yes, of course it's possible. But it's about as practical as taking the sand from a local beach to make a pair of glasses. The process from living tree to usable lumber is almost as complex as from lumber to finished project. It starts with the correct way to fell a tree, so as not to damage it. Then you have to find a way to cut the logs into boards, either with a portable sawmill or by taking the log to a mill. Then you need to dry it, a process that can take years.

So milling your own lumber is a lot of trouble, but there are times it's worth it—such

as for a well-loved tree. Such was the case with the wood for this jewelry box. It was a venerable maple that came down in a storm; a much beloved backyard tree on which the owner's kids had grown up swinging. The owner couldn't stand to see the tree ground up and turned to mulch. So this jewelry box is the sixth piece made from its wood.

It may be a long process, but it's not an impossible one. A good place to start for information is the book *Taunton's Complete Illustrated Guide to Working with Wood* by Andy Rae (The Taunton Press, Inc. 2005). It will give you the details necessary to do each of these steps right.

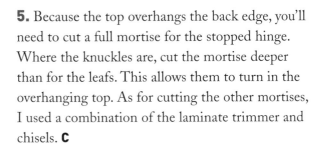

CUT A DEEPER MORTISE just where the hinge knuckles will lie. This allows the hinge to pivot freely with an overhanging top.

FIT THE SIDE DOORS between the posts, then measure the height to cut to length.

5. Because the top overhangs the back edge, you'll need to cut a full mortise for the stopped hinge. Where the knuckles are, cut the mortise deeper than for the leafs. This allows them to turn in the overhanging top. As for cutting the other mortises, I used a combination of the laminate trimmer and chisels. **C**

Fitting the Doors

With the sides of the top fitted (though not glued) in place, you have an actual space to fit the doors.

1. Clamp the top sides in place and measure the opening. If necessary, cut your doors to fit the space, making them slightly smaller (by about $1/8$ in.) on each side. The two doors on this box came out to be $5^7/16$ in. by $10^3/16$ in.

2. Rip to width first, making sure the sides are parallel. If your box is slightly off-square, make your doors off-square to fit. Use a block plane to shave the door edge at a slight angle if necessary.

3. Crosscut the doors at the angle that will make them parallel to the bottom and top (not always exactly 90 degrees). **A**

4. Lay out the knife-hinge mortises centered and flush with the ends of the upper and lower edges of the doors. Remember to set the hinges on the left side of one door and the right side of the other door. Use a marking gauge to scribe the sides of each mortise. Make them square with an open end. **B**

SCRIBE THE HINGE LOCATIONS on the ends of the doors with a marking gauge.

5. Cut the waste from each mortise with a laminate trimmer. This job is relatively difficult because the trimmer must balance on the edge of the thin door. You can clamp the door to a bench edge or larger block of wood for support if you prefer.

6. Pare the mortise edges flush until the hinge leaf fits in place. Take very small cuts with gingerly taps of the mallet. Because you're cutting into end grain, the chance of splitting off a chunk of the face is high. I clamp the doors together for no other reason than it saves a bit of time taking them in and out of the vise. **C**

7. Sand the outside edge of the door to the radius of the hinge. This will allow the door to open. How much to take off is hard to say. It largely depends on the location of your hinges, so test fit the door in place. Remove only as much of the edge as

necessary to let the door open freely. I don't set the hinges in place with screws for this process, as it's not necessary. Only after finishing and before assembly do I set the screws. **D & E**

8. Add door stops to the inside top corner of the necklace compartment where the door will meet the edge. Size their length, about 1³⁄₁₆ in., so the doors

SAND A QUARTER RADIUS on the edge of each door on a stationary belt sander, matching the radius of the knife-hinge end.

PARE THE HINGE-MORTISE CORNERS clean with a chisel. If you use a mallet go easy because it's easy to split the end grain.

TEST THE SANDED RADIUS with the door in place to see if it clears the post when the door is open.

GLUE AND CLAMP the door stops in place, flush with the top of the box.

stop when they're parallel with the bottom edge of the box. Make them a bit shorter and later you can add a rubber cushion on the end for a muted sound. **F**

Making the Drawer Boxes

The jewelry box has three drawers and a compartment hidden by two false drawer fronts. Joint the drawer boxes however you like—with rabbets, nails, or super-fancy dovetails. As jewelry boxes are special, I tend to go for the dovetails to keep things in harmony. After all, you wouldn't want to let your sweetie think she's not worth the extra few hours of labor. For more details about cutting dovetails, see Chapter 3 (p. 35).

1. Mill up drawer stock, ¼ in. thick. Cut all fronts and backs to length. Check the measurements on the chart against your actual box opening, and opt for the latter if they're different.

2. On the tablesaw, rip a ⅛-in. kerf on the inside faces of all the drawer sides for where the bottom panel will go. It should be about ⅛ in. or ³⁄₁₆ in. from the bottom edge. **A**

3. As you have three identical drawer boxes to make, give each group of parts a letter or number on the top edge to keep them straight. Also mark each of the corner joints. The groove will help remind you which is the inside face. **B**

work
SMART

When you lay out the tails, be sure the half pin at the bottom isn't above the groove. If it is, the groove will show on the side of the finished box.

RIP ⅛-IN.-WIDE GROOVES in the drawer box sides on the tablesaw for the drawer bottoms.

MARK EACH SET OF DRAWER box sides to avoid confusion during assembly—letters in the middle to indicate the set and numbers at the ends to indicate the corner joint.

SAW ALL OF THE TAIL BOARDS at once to save time and help keep the cuts square to the faces of the boards.

FINISH THE INSIDES of the drawer boxes before assembly. Tape over the joints so you don't get finish on them.

4. Cut all the tails at the same time. It's faster and also helps keep your line of cut at 90 degrees to the sides. **C**

5. Cut matching pins for each set and fit each joint. See Chapter 3 for more details (p. 38).

6. Finish-sand the interior faces of all the drawer sides. Be sure to finish them before assembly because the box bottoms will be lined. It's nearly impossible to finish the insides of the boxes after assembly without getting finish on the lining. Avoid

CUT PIECES OF SELF-ADHERING felt exactly the size of the drawer bottoms. Stick them on before assembly.

getting any finish on the joinery, as it will interfere with glue adhesion. **D**

7. Apply felt lining to the box bottoms. The drawer bottoms don't need to be sanded, but they should be dusted off first. Cut self-adhering felt pieces to size and stick them on. **E**

8. Glue and assemble the drawer boxes. When the glue has dried, finish-sand the exterior, including the top and bottom edges.

9. Test the drawers in their slots. If they're slightly too big, sand down the faces a bit until they glide in and out smoothly.

LINING WITH FELT

When ferrous metals, mainly iron and steel, come in prolonged contact with wood, they tend to rust. So if you're planning on storing anything of that sort in the box, you need to line it. Self-adhesive felt works very well, is sold by the sheet, and looks great. One 1-ft. by 2-ft. sheet is enough for this box. For best results, apply it to box bottoms before assembly. Otherwise trimming it to fit and sticking it in place neatly is nearly impossible. Leather also works very well (see Chapter 4 for how to apply leather lining, p. 54).

Making Drawer Fronts

The drawer fronts make a sizeable portion of the front of the box, so choose a nice piece of wood. If you're really organized, you could make the two front face pieces from the same piece and give the whole front a very uniform look. But as the drawer fronts stand proud of the front faces, I think the different grain looks as good if not better. The drawer fronts are thicker than the front faces. They stand proud for a simple and nice detail.

1. Size and trim the board for the drawer fronts the same way you did for the doors. The fronts should

A

CUT A SHALLOW KERF in the false front to make it look like two drawers.

be about $1/32$ in. to $1/16$ in. thinner than the opening between the front faces.

2. Measure on the actual box to determine the height of each drawer front. Just be careful not to overlap a front with the runners of the drawer above. Crosscut them to length on the tablesaw. In this box, the lowest drawer front is $2^5/16$ in. high, the middle drawer front is $2^3/16$ in. high, and the top drawer is 2 in. high. The false front is $3^9/16$ in. high.

3. The false front should look like two drawers that haven't been sawn completely in half. Simply saw a shallow kerf with a fine-toothed handsaw where you want to create the visual divide. Cut about $1/4$ in. deep. I cut a kerf $1^{15}/16$ in. from the bottom, so the topmost drawer looks $1^9/16$ in. tall. **A**

4. Finish-sand the drawer fronts.

Attaching the Drawer Fronts

The traditional way to attach drawer fronts is with screws from the inside of the drawer box. However, I find that gluing ones this small is easier. The trouble is that you can't adjust them later. So make any adjustments immediately, before the glue dries. Start with the bottom drawer and work up.

1. Remove the top two drawers.

2. Glue and clamp the bottom drawer front to the drawer box while it's in place. Use a piece of paper to raise the drawer front just a hair off the bottom of the box to ensure smooth running. Center it by eye. **A**

3. When the glue has dried, repeat the process for the next drawer up. The third drawer is hardest to align because you need to pull the drawer out to clamp it. **B**

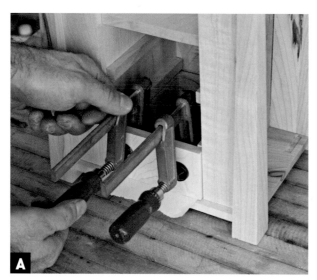

GLUE AND CLAMP THE BOTTOM DRAWER FRONT to the drawer box. Set the drawer box in place to get the alignment just right.

GLUE AND CLAMP the second drawer in the same fashion as the first.

Attaching the False Front

To make the false drawer front fit tightly between the front faces, you need to add a strip of veneer on both sides. You can't really make them out of wider stock, because then they won't look the same width as the real drawer fronts.

1. Cut two strips of veneer about ¼ in. wide and glue them to the back edges of both sides of the false front. If you don't have veneer, rip very thin strips off a wider board on your tablesaw. **A**

2. Press the false front in place. If it's too tight, sand down one edge. If it's loose, add another strip of veneer.

3. When the fit is snug, apply a little glue to the edges and clamp in place (across the front posts).

GLUE VENEER STRIPS along the back edge of both sides of the false front for a snug fit between the front faces.

Finishing

This box is a little odd in that you want to finish it largely before final gluing of the tops onto the frame. The reason is that the knife hinges get captured.

1. The box will tend to pick up a few dents and scratches as you build it. Now is the time to hunt them all down and steam or sand them out. Maple can take a high level of polish, so I'd certainly finish-sand to 220-grit and possibly higher.

2. I finished the box with a wiping varnish. Finish everything at this point, being very careful to avoid the dowel holes on the top and the interior of the lined drawers. Let the finish set and cure.

3. Now, finally, set the knife hinges in place on the doors and in the box parts. Drill ⅜-in.-deep pilot holes for the screws to avoid splitting.

4. Press the necklace hooks in place with a tiny dab of epoxy at the ends. This is easier to do before you attach the top sides.

5. Clamp the tops in place with the doors captured. Use a rag or block to avoid marring the top when clamping. **A**

Setting the Hardware

1. Drill centered pilot holes for the drawer pulls. Use the same pulls for the doors on the sides.

2. Set the hinges for the center of the top and attach it. It should not touch the top sides as you raise and lower it. Shim the hinges to prevent this, if necessary.

3. If you like, add padded ring bars to one or more of the drawers. They come in 25-in. lengths and can be cut down to any size.

4. Add felt pads to the bottom of the box posts.

GLUE AND CLAMP the tops to the box with the doors captured. Adjust the clamps as necessary to get them to sit flat and straight.

Metric Conversion Chart

Inches	Centimeters	Millimeters	Inches	Centimeters	Millimeters
1/8	0.3	3	13	33.0	330
1/4	0.6	6	14	35.6	356
3/8	1.0	10	15	38.1	381
1/2	1.3	13	16	40.6	406
5/8	1.6	16	17	43.2	432
3/4	1.9	19	18	45.7	457
7/8	2.2	22	19	48.3	483
1	2.5	25	20	50.8	508
1 1/4	3.2	32	21	53.3	533
1 1/2	3.8	38	22	55.9	559
1 3/4	4.4	44	23	58.4	584
2	5.1	51	24	61.0	610
2 1/2	6.4	64	25	63.5	635
3	7.6	76	26	66.0	660
3 1/2	8.9	89	27	68.6	686
4	10.2	102	28	71.1	711
4 1/2	11.4	114	29	73.7	737
5	12.7	127	30	76.2	762
6	15.2	152	31	78.7	787
7	17.8	178	32	81.3	813
8	20.3	203	33	83.8	838
9	22.9	229	34	86.4	864
10	25.4	254	35	88.9	889
11	27.9	279	36	91.4	914
12 1/2	30.5	305			

Resources

American Woodcrafters Supply Co.

212 East Main P.O. Box G
Riceville, IA 50466
800-995-4032
www.americanwoodcrafterssupply.com

BC Specialties

2167 May Court
Simi Valley, CA 93063
888-886-8220
www.bcspecialties.com

Brusso

20 Vandam Street
New York, NY 10013
212-337-8510
www.brusso.com

Rockler

4365 Willow Dr.
Medina, MN 55340
800-279-4441
www.rockler.com

Whitechapel Ltd.

P.O. Box 11719
Jackson, WY 83002
800-468-5534
www.whitechapel-ltd.com

Woodcraft

P.O. Box 1686
406 Airport Industrial Park Road
Parkersburg, WV 26102
800-225-1153
www.woodcraft.com

Woodworker's Supply

1108 North Glenn Road
Casper, WY 82601
307-237-5354
www.woodworker.com

Index